Hudom, the new
Bamboo Forest employee...
was a spy all along?!

"For sure.
We think he just
sells information."

By the Grace of the Gods ·11·

The nine gods pile onto Ryoma as soon as he is summoned to them...

Wilieris

Ryoma
Takebayashi

Serelipta

Each of their outfits were accented by large pearls. Their appearance and poise caused some murmuring among the other participants.

By the Grace of the Gods

Roy
Illustrations by Ririnra

BY THE GRACE OF THE GODS VOLUME 11
by Roy

Translated by Adam Seacord
Edited by Nathan Redmond
Layout by Jennifer Elgabrowny
English Front Cover and Lettering by Macaran
English Print Cover by Kelsey Denton

Copyright © 2021 Roy
Illustrations by Ririnra

First published in Japan in 2021
Publication rights for this English edition arranged through Hobby Japan, Tokyo.

Find more books like this one at www.j-novel.club!

Managing Director: Samuel Pinansky
Light Novel Line Manager: Chi Tran
Managing Editor: Jan Mitsuko Cash
Managing Translator: Kristi Fernandez
QA Manager: Hannah N. Carter
Marketing Manager: Stephanie Hii
Project Manager: Kristine Johnson

ISBN: 978-1-7183-5390-9
Printed in Korea
First Printing: December 2022
10 9 8 7 6 5 4 3 2 1

Contents

Contents

⌁ Chapter 7 Episode 21 ⌁
The Days Are Changing

The next morning, I braved the gloomy overcast sky and razor-sharp, icy wind and headed to the security company to review any news and tasks for the day. The first item on my agenda was a package that had been delivered from Serge; Lilian brought it in for me.

"Here you are," Lilian said as she handed it to me. "It's my understanding that this is the magical item you ordered, Master Ryoma."

That said, I'd ordered so many magical items from Serge that her lack of specificity didn't help narrow it down. Opening the box, I found it to be a pressure cooker, a familiar modern-day kitchen appliance.

"Finally," I remarked. This was something I had ordered from Dinome, the magical item maker, some time ago. I had been cautioned that this order would take a while, since it presented new challenges to deal with, such as keeping a proper airtight seal and ensuring durability, not to mention all the safety procedures. But now, it was finally mine!

"Couldn't have come a moment sooner either." The cold was getting especially bitter now, and I had found myself repeatedly wishing for one of these to have in the kitchen. I had to hand it to Dinome for getting this project done on time in the dead of winter.

"Oh? Master Ryoma, there's a letter at the bottom of the box."

"Really? Let me see… Hm, that's interesting."

"How so?"

"Hm… It says that he's never done anything like this before, so he wants me to give some feedback. Also, he wants more of the rubber that I had provided as raw material for the whole project, and a few other things, so he'd like me to stop by for a chat when I have the time. I mean, content-wise, it's pretty standard, but his writing style is strangely quaint…"

Not to criticize his skill or anything, though. We exchanged letters quite frequently regarding magical items for use in the kitchen. I figured that he couldn't put anything confidential in a letter like this.

"Doesn't sound like he wants me there in a hurry, but I think I'll stop by sometime soon when my schedule allows."

"Understood. I'll rearrange our itinerary a bit so you'll have time for that."

"Thank you."

Then came two decently thick piles of paperwork.

"These are reports from the construction department and the city clerk."

"Right…"

Our construction department was composed of the people working on rezoning the slums, centered around the thirty veterans of the trade whom Zeph had rounded up the day I demolished the first orphanage. Back when I had them help me rebuild the new orphanage, I explained my 3D printer-like magical construction method, and had them focus on the building process. Now I'd split them up into groups of five and get them to train the new hires to aid in the rezoning as foremen and chiefs. I was sure this would be easier on the newer recruits, since they'd sooner take orders from someone who looked to be above them than from a child.

"Things at the construction department are going smoothly; they're on track to complete the current task on schedule... Right, I'll get the next site ready. Might be as soon as this afternoon... Now, the city's been working on guiding and assigning lodging for the homeless. Maybe I should prioritize housing for the city next? We have the land for that, so..."

I sketched up my proposed schedule on a piece of paper, which I'd get both our construction department and someone from the city to review.

Once I get the green light, I'll demolish the old buildings, prepare the lot, and gather materials for the construction at the same time with magic. Thanks to our division of labor, the rezoning and renovations were moving along quickly. With the winter getting more intense, we could expect ever-increasing levels of cold and frequent precipitation. Those were conditions liable to get people living on the streets killed, so I hoped the workers would manage as many projects as they feasibly could without it affecting their well-being.

"And...there. Go deliver this letter for me, would you? Since there seems to be nothing urgent today, I'll head over to the Adventurers' Guild, since I've been meaning to go there."

"Yes, sir."

And so, out into the cold I stepped, and off to the Adventurers' Guild I went. Lately, I hadn't needed to do so much running around the city. Even today, once I was done with my meeting at the Adventurers' Guild, I was pretty much free until the afternoon, when I'd be working at the construction sites. My workload would more than likely plummet in due time, and I would be able to spend most of my days improving myself through study or training.

Not that I was unhappy with that prospect, but I also felt a twinge of sadness knowing that this sudden glut of work and productivity, for whatever it was worth, was going to come to an end…

While pondering over how this may have been the workaholic in me doing the talking, I arrived at the Adventurers' Guild and opened the front door to the sight of a group of men shouting at each other.

"You wot?!"

"Shut yer damn trap!"

"You got a problem with that?! Wanna go?!"

"Yeah, let's fight!"

"Them's fightin' words!"

Apparently, two groups of six ruffians apiece, one of humans and one of beastkin, were having a disagreement. The few receptionists and male employees of the guild came running out, calling for them to stand down, to no avail. A brawl seemed imminent until…

"QUIET!"

An enraged voice rang out; it belonged to the guildmaster, Worgan. Even over the noise of the crowd, you could pick his voice out instantly.

"Ah, crap."

"There's the former S-rank."

"Hmph…"

The men immediately fell silent.

"Really, gentlemen, where's the fire in your bellies gone? If there's something on your weak minds, spit it out," urged the guildmaster.

"Nothing."

"We were just having a conversation."

Men from both groups began muttering excuses; the guildmaster's scorn had evidently done the trick. It seemed the men were neither brave nor stupid enough to defy the guildmaster, but they still looked visibly disgruntled. They all appeared to be in their twenties.

Worgan answered with a sigh. "I'm going to have you all exclusively do supervised chore quests for a little while. I want to see you all in this guild at this time every day for that."

"You wot?! We ain't even taken a job yet!"

"Yeah! You're not the boss of us! We decide what quests we wanna do!"

Of course, they all complained about that.

"Very well," the guildmaster answered without hesitation. "If you hate the idea that much, you don't have to come in tomorrow, or the next day, or ever again! By my authority as guildmaster, your adventurer licenses are now revoked, and you're all expelled from this guild!"

"Th-That's not fair!"

"You ain't playin' fair!"

"Shut up! That's my final word. You'd better do some long, hard thinking about all the stunts you've pulled by tomorrow. If you still have a problem with it, then don't bother showing your faces in here again. Now, you're done for the day, so get your sorry hides home and stay out of trouble."

The men finally shuffled away under the weight of Worgan's authority.

"Hm? Oh, hi, Ryoma! Didn't see you there!" He called out to me with a smile. Naturally, all eyes in the guild were on me.

"Good morning. I just got here."

"All right. I still have some paperwork to sort out, so I'll have to ask you to wait a few minutes before our meeting."

Of course, a guildmaster would have been working with some confidential documents. I told him there was no problem and that

I would wait here until I was called. Worgan retreated, and the other employees of the guild returned to their posts. I was thinking of ways to kill a few minutes when I heard some comments coming from the group of human men, accompanied by unabashed staring.

"What's that kid doing here?"

"How should I know?"

"The hell is this, a playground?"

"Well, he ain't carrying, but I heard the guildmaster wanted to see him, so he must be an adventurer."

"Must've screwed up somehow. The job's stopped so he's not wearing any gear."

"With the way the guildmaster greeted him? Yeah, right."

Even the beastkin were grumbling about me.

"They seemed really close."

"The kid's wearing good clothes."

"Maybe he gets all the easy money quests."

"Nepotism at its finest, I tell ya…"

"And we're always getting the short end of the stick."

"No ranking up for us."

This seemed like a bit of a problem. I had a hunch they had something to do with what I was about to discuss with the guildmaster…

"Ryoma, the guildmaster is ready to see you." Maylene, the receptionist of the guild who often helped me out, called me in.

"Thank you. I'll go in now." I made my way to the guildmaster's office.

"Sorry for the wait," Worgan said upon my arrival.

"It's no problem. I was just watching things unfold."

Once Worgan gestured for me to sit on the sofa, I obliged and told him about what had happened.

"Right… Those dimwits."

"I'm not sure if they plan to do anything to me, but I suppose I *did* leave quite the impression. So, why did you purposely direct your attention to me?"

Unless I was mistaken, Worgan's face when he greeted me had been shaded with a hint of mischief, and I could see it again when I pointed this out.

"You know why I called you here, right?"

"About cleaning the drains around the city."

This was the gist of what I had been told so far: It will start to rain and snow heavily in the city for a while, so there's a quest to clean and check up on all of the drains laid out throughout the city. Some delinquent adventurers will be taking on the quest as punishment, and the guildmaster needed someone he could trust to supervise them. The letter mentioned that he wanted to discuss my role in the quest too.

"You mentioned jobs tomorrow, so I assume those were the adventurers we're putting to work."

"Some of them, anyway… I'm sure you've heard that the influx of workers in the city's been causing headaches for us too."

"Guess you can't catch a break, huh. Who are those adventurers, anyway?"

"Some rubes from the countryside who got it into their skulls that since they could fight better than anyone else in their little villages, they can't do wrong in the big city."

"They definitely have chutzpah. Plus I get the feeling they overestimate their own abilities."

"They used to take care of nuisance animals in their hometown, so they have some combat experience there. Talent's not bad. They'd be decent if they'd only check their egos and train hard,

15

but that's never going to happen at this rate." The guildmaster sighed. "Sorry, I'm just griping about my job to you."

"Don't worry about it, I can lend you an ear anytime."

Worgan laughed. "In that case, you'll have to join me in a drink sometime."

"Deal."

His expression became stoic again. "Back to business. I'll be there for the cleaning job too, starting the day after tomorrow, and there'll be other supervisors on duty, but the work is going to be done by a bunch of rubes just like the ones you saw out there. They do nothing but gripe and start fights. It seems to me that some of them will no doubt try to start something with you under the supes' noses. So if any of them try to screw with you at any time, you have my permission to give them a proper ass-kicking."

Wow, uh, didn't expect that.

"They've got it coming to them. We've already given them enough verbal warnings. I'm sure a good, solid whack to their bloated egos would do them a bit of good… Adventurers or not, if they keep this up, it'll land 'em all in the can."

Worgan looked intimidating on the surface, but cared well for his adventurers. However, it sounded like he was out of patience if they caused trouble again. These certainly didn't look like the kind of people who'd listen to reason.

"Of course, I can defend myself if it comes to that. Shouldn't be an issue."

"Thanks. When we get the chance, that drink's on my tab."

After that, we went over the cleaning process and schedule to improve efficiency, considering which drains needed to be cleaned first or which sections would take the longest time.

"Going by the rain and snow records from the last few years, we should be able to get this done pretty quickly," I noted.

"Yep. We've been getting absolutely dumped on in winter lately, drains have been clogging from the trash on the street and flooding the city. I want to get this done before the weather gets really bad, so it's all down to you and your slimes, Ryoma."

"That's what we do. Plus, after all you've done for me, this is the least I can do. See you around." With the meeting wrapped up, I turned to leave.

"Wait a second," Worgan called. Had I forgotten to mention something? "You got a weapon on you? Not that you'd have trouble taking them on without one."

I was wearing my suit since the meeting was the only thing on my schedule. It might have looked like I wasn't wearing any armor or carrying a weapon. "Thank you for your concern, but I'll be fine." Reaching for my belt, I grabbed a portion of the buckle and drew my iron slime, which instantly formed itself into a sword.

"In your *belt*?"

"Back when I lived in the forest, I used to make clothes from the hides of my game, so something like this is pretty easy. I'm sure you've noticed that I have been a bit paranoid recently; this was one of my projects."

In India, there's a martial art called *kalaripayattu* which involves the use of a thin and flexible steel sword called an *urumi*. In China, they used to use a sword in much the same way, sheathing it in their belt. The iron slime formed a relatively soft metal, which wasn't ideal for ordinary swords, but perfectly suited for turning into an *urumi* or belt sword because of how flexible it was. With the slime's Harden skill and my own energy meditation, it could be hardened to use as a normal sword after drawing it from my belt. A very convenient weapon and partner to have with me at all times.

"You were pretty wound up until those people came from the duke's... Is that bracelet you've been wearing on your arm a weapon too? Just thought you were accessorizing, but you started wearing that when things were getting tense."

Good eye. I had a wire slime on my wrist, disguised as a bracelet, allowing me to use it as a *kusari-fundo* if need be, using the gem as the weight on the end of the chain. I could also use it as a gauntlet, or even to tie someone down. Another very useful slime.

"Do you have any more on you?"

"No, these are the only two I can use as weapons. I am wearing a blade-proof undershirt and trousers, both made from tough silk. My shoes have a sort of steel toe, made from the hardening solution of a sticky slime."

I also planned to mass-produce any of these that could be used by any of my new employees as safety measures.

"So you're pretty much fully geared up in all but looks."

"Embarrassing as it is, I was kind of a wreck... I've calmed down now, but still, may as well use what I have. After all, I still need to watch my back."

"Well, I do have my concerns...and they're not about your gear."

Still, Worgan left it at that.

Once I left the guild, the group of adventurers started tailing me without even trying to hide it, so I lured them into an alley and gave them a proper ass-kicking. I reminded them to show up to the cleaning job the next day and made them get their wounds treated at the security company before letting them go home.

~ Chapter 7 Episode 22 ~
First Snow

I was awoken by the brisk air and walked outside into a winter wonderland. The weather outside must have been frightful...

"What am I thinking? They don't have those songs here," I muttered to myself. My current location was my humble abode within the abandoned mines a few hours north of Gimul. Of course, I was the only human around, which meant there was no one to shovel the snow piled at my door this morning, which seemed to be two or three inches deep. I'd been to Hokkaido on business and it certainly wasn't anything like the tundra I'd seen there, but this would still make walking a tad inconvenient.

"If I don't get a move on, I'm gonna be late... Guess I'll pull out the old ace." I hadn't had situations like this in mind when I came up with the aforementioned ace, but what the hey, it was worth a shot.

Half an hour later, I was lying on the ground in a patch of woods near the northern gate to Gimul.

"It worked... It actually worked! This definitely makes long-distance teleportation to places I've already visited a lot easier. Of course, it does require some caution when you're getting out of it, but looks like the snow doesn't affect how it works."

I had done some experiments with another combination of slimes and magic, like those I'd already done with the stone, weed, and sand slimes. I had been trying to come up with more combos for a few days now. In reality, though, all I did was put a stone slime in the woods with enough rocks to keep it fed for a while. Examples of space magic included the basic Teleport, the intermediate Warp, and the advanced Gate; that last one was still beyond my purview.

Sebas, the master of space magic, once told me that these three spells were essentially the same, their only differences being the distance I could travel and the magic expenditure involved. Under his tutelage, I had learned to cast Warp, so of course, I tried to see if I could learn Gate while I was at it. Turns out that jumping to an area out of your sight is a lot more difficult than I expected it would be. It used to be that I could only use Teleport to end up a few feet away; with Warp, I could travel further, but only as far away as my eyes could see. Maybe because I was relying too heavily on my eyesight without realizing it, I could never jump to anywhere I couldn't see. I felt like I could jump in the direction of my choice just by pouring more magic into a Teleport spell, but decided against this method. It would be a terrible hassle at the very least, and I could have wound up dead if I had proceeded with it and ended up getting stuck in a rock or something.

That's why I came up with this method of jumping to a slime I had set up at a location before. Because of our contract, I could communicate with familiars even when they were far away. Even at a distance where we couldn't communicate, I could feel their direction and distance from me, so I just had to jump towards it. The process felt like fast traveling in an RPG. This new magic application allowed me to practically jump into the city, drastically reducing my commute time. Quite a productive morning, considering the other potential applications of this spell. With my thoughts wandering, I walked through the northern gate.

■　■　■

Having gained some extra time from the jump, I decided to stop by the laundry shop, making my way past people on the streets starting to shovel the snow here and there. When I arrived, my employees were all lined up in front of the shop.

"Good morning!" I called as I came closer, and they responded in kind.

"What are you doing here so early, sir?" Carme asked in surprise.

"I wanted to come check on the shop since it snowed." I wasn't worried since we had discussed the protocol in case of snow, but I wanted to make a little tour since I had extra time.

"No, I meant… How early did you leave the northern mines to make it here this early through the snow?"

Right. Without explaining my new commute method, they would think that I was leaving my place at a ridiculously early hour. I explained *how* I got there early.

"Oh, good. I thought you were trying something crazy again," Carme said.

"I think it's pretty crazy that he's casting advanced magic at his age…"

I felt nostalgic at Hudom's surprise, now that the other employees had stopped being shocked at every little thing I did.

"Good morning!"

"Hey, Ryoma!"

The family next door called out to me.

"Good morning! Shoveling some snow?"

"Snow's not good for safety or business unless you shovel it often."

"The kids are ecstatic about it, but it's tough work for us every winter…"

Sieg the butcher and Pauline the florist turned around to watch their children, Rick and Renny, play in the fresh snow.

"Brr! It's cold…"

"Oh, Sieg. I have just the spell… Sunlight!"

With my incantation, a ball of light materialized ten feet or so above us, and I could immediately feel my body warm up at the touch of the light. It had been a while since I cast it, but the spell went off without a hitch.

"Ooh, that's pretty warm."

"It's a spell meant to emulate daylight that I've made by combining light and fire magic."

There was another spell that could have served as a light source ("Light") cast by only using the light element, but Light didn't carry heat. I had created this spell because I wanted to try and simulate the warmth of the sun. This spell alone could warm you as much as sitting under clear daylight, but combining it with barrier magic that shuts out the wind and the cold, it became a very useful heater substitute in the forest over winter.

"I'll set up a few of them where you can take breaks. Make sure to stay warm. The cold isn't good for you." There was another spell called Space Heater, but that could have led to burns and fires so I decided against it. Even in the forest, Sunlight or a simple bonfire got me through most days, so I wasn't worried about it.

For good measure, though, I decided to distribute hand warmers of my own concoction. "These are my prototypes, so please feel free to use them. It would be a great help if you could give me feedback on them later."

"Thank you."

"My hands and feet are starting to freeze up. This looks nice and easy."

My first impression told me that the warmers were a hit with the ladies, as Fina, Jane, Maria, Sheruma the chef, and even Lilyn gathered around to discuss the best place to keep the warmer on them. On the other hand, the men didn't seem to have much of a strong opinion on the matter, as they took them and shoved them into their pockets.

"I've been experimenting with other items, and I still have plenty of ideas to work on with my slime experiments. Please let me know if you ever need anything. I would love to have you test some of my other prototypes."

Salt could prevent some snow from piling, but I was considering making a melting agent and antifreeze like calcium chloride with alchemy. My concern would be with the salinity of the earth, but that shouldn't be a problem in the city... Unless the drainage causes some damage to the environment. Would alcohol be safer? It's the main component in antifreeze used in cars, so it should be able to melt thin layers of frost or ice. I could use alcohol that drunk slimes produce along with any alcoholic drinks that didn't turn out as well. If the temperature was high enough that it wouldn't refreeze, a pour of water would do the trick. I could make boiling water by mixing fire and water magic, and combining wind magic with that would make hot steam. Well, if I was going to use magic, maybe it'd be more effective to lower the freezing point of the snow pile and clean that up? On the other hand, I could turn the snow into chunks of ice, peeling them off the ground and getting rid of them as is.

I remembered that some places in Hokkaido employ snow-melting equipment that utilizes well or stream water. While I couldn't modify the drainage system of the city or anything, I could set up a temporary solution with the help of the slimes, especially that one that'd newly evolved. I was starting to get the hang of evolving slimes, lately. With more free time away from work and the team of goblins I was keeping, continuous experimentation had become a reality, allowing much more varied and expeditious results.

"Sir... I'm glad you're enjoying yourself, but are you watching the time? I thought you said you had several stops to make."

"Oh, cra—"

Dolce was right! I felt bad that I couldn't stay and help, but I decided to take my leave. I was announcing my departure when Ox called to me, Fay by his side.

"All I can do is wield the sword. But you can always tell me if anything needs to be done. I am your slave, after all. Of course, you've never treated me as such. Still, I owe you a debt for allowing me to take up the sword again."

"I'm sure everyone's told you to take it easy..." Fay chimed in. "I'll make the shop do just fine without you. Of course, we'd be in trouble if you *never* came back; the shop still needs you. So call us if you need anything. Got it?"

The other employees were nodding along behind them. It was reassuring to know that I was leaving the laundry shop in good hands, as expected.

"Thank you. I'll ask for more training for testing my prototypes."

With my trusty crew sending me off, I finally headed to my next destination.

■ ■ ■

After touring some spots around the city, when the sun was high in the sky, I made my way to the Adventurers' Guild. I had gone to the security company, the garbage plant, construction sites...

At each detour, I received words of encouragement from the people I'd met.

I came to realize that a business run by a child my age was a rare enough occurrence for people to talk about it. Apparently, I was pretty well known among the laundry shop patrons, notably among housewives. After my return from Fatoma, my actions had compounded my fame in Gimul. By now, complete strangers had begun to notice and greet me. Many of them told me that they saw me cleaning the drainage system, followed by comments of thanks or concern that the adventurers I was working with were giving me a hard time. Yet again, I felt gratitude for the people of Gimul. Their concerns about the delinquent adventurers, however, were entirely unfounded.

"Good morning."

"L-Line it up!"

"G-Good morning, Boss!"

"Wh-When you say it like that..."

Somehow, they had started to treat me like their godfather... Where did I go wrong?

⤳ Chapter 7 Episode 23 ⤳
With the Delinquent Adventurers

One little greeting was all it took for the team of delinquent adventurers waiting before the guild to line up single file in a perfect salute. Naturally, such a display in the middle of the city garnered the attention of all passersby. Their gazes boring into me, I hurried over to Darson's establishment with my lackeys in tow.

"Good morning!" I called out to Darson, who was shoveling snow out front as we arrived.

"There you are. Come on in."

Darson planted his shovel in a mound of snow and let us in.

"Darson, could we take a look at your merchandise?"

"Be my guest."

"Thank you." I turned to the adventurers. "Please pick out a weapon of your choice. Handle them with care."

"Yes, Boss!"

"And be quiet."

"Yes, Boss," they answered, slightly less loudly. I was never going to get used to this...

Then, Darson called from behind the counter. "They're those slacker adventurers I've been hearing about? Worgan told me what's up. Looks like you're handling them pretty well."

"Do you think so? They don't fight me on things, at least."

"Those wannabe rebels just do what they're told; that's enough of an accomplishment. They're even calling you 'Boss.'"

"I feel like I've just scared them into submission. And they apparently think I'm *older* than them... Some races don't look like their age, right?"

"I think I get it. You're not exactly childlike. More of a geezer, if I had to pick."

"What?!" Me?! My youthful eleven-year-old self...?! I guess my gut reaction aged me in and of itself. With the mind of a middle-aged man, I couldn't put my whole heart into denying this assessment.

"Why are you giving those guys weapons? You're paying for them, right?"

"I ruined all of their weapons on our first day working together."

That day, I had lured them into a deserted alley when they picked a fight with me. I had mercilessly defeated them as instructed by the guildmaster.

"I kind of egged them on. A lot."

At first, I was taking care of them hand to hand, but they were more stubborn than I had expected. Worse still, they gave me dumb excuses like "I was just going easy on you." So, I kept casting healing magic on them to fight them over and over, crushing their excuses one at a time.

"Eventually, I made them use their weapons...and they got broken. Those were their property and tools to earn their livelihood. Even though they started our skirmish, I encouraged them to use their weapons, and they ended up breaking, so I think it's right that I replace them."

"Did you need to come with them, though? Most people would just hand them some cash."

"There's something I wanted to see."

"Wanted to see?"

"It seemed like many of their weapons weren't the best fit for them. For example…" I spotted one of them who had just picked out a greatsword.

"Beno."

"Yes, Boss! What can I do for you?"

"That's very similar to the sword you had."

"Oh, yes. I figured I'd try to find one like my old one."

"Can you show me your stance, please? No need to swing the sword."

Looking a little confused, Beno complied. The tip of his sword, however, was slightly quivering from its own weight. I remembered him looking like he was being swung by his sword during our previous skirmish.

"Gotcha. This isn't the sword for your body type. I recommended picking a lighter greatsword, switching to a longsword that you could still swing with both hands or a blunt weapon that weighs the same. If you really want to use a sword this weight, you better put on a little more muscle, first," Darson explained.

"There you have it," I chimed in.

"Really?"

"Darson is an expert on weapons, and an adventurer giant who walked before you. He was once an S-rank, after all. He worked with the current guildmaster Worgan."

All dozen of the young adventurers turned at us in surprise, apparently learning Darson's impressive background for the first time.

"I haven't been S-rank for a long time," Darson answered. "That doesn't mean I don't know what I'm talking about. If you can't keep your sword straight, it won't cut. Regardless of size. But you're far from the only rookie who needs to hear this."

"Is there a special reason why you chose the greatsword?" I asked.

"Not really... I'd only been using it because I found an old one in a dusty shed back home."

"In that case, I recommend changing your weapon now. It's your choice to make since it'll affect your life and livelihood. And make sure to take the guild's training. Knowing one thing about how to use your weapon could save your life."

"Y-Yes, sir."

At Darson's advice, he began looking at swords suited for single- and doublehanded use, as well as war hammers and the like.

"Excuse me, Boss. I'm good at carving up game, so I've been using a hunting knife as my weapon in combat as well. What do you think?" One of the others came over.

I advised him on what I could tell, and had Darson chime in with his expertise. Before I knew it, we had gone through all of the adventurers to help them pick out their new weapons.

"Everyone is confident in their choice, now?"

"Yes, Boss!"

"Can we check out, please, Darson?"

"Yeah. Give me a sec."

Darson quickly calculated our total, and I handed over the cash. With our shopping trip coming to an end, the adventurers quickly became sulky.

Darson asked, "What's with the long faces all of a sudden?"

"Must be because we're about to test their new weapons and get in some training." They would have to grow accustomed to their new weapons, of course. After this, we would head to the security company and continue training in an unused spot on the premises. For their training, however, they would use a metal slime shaped

31

and weighted to resemble their weapons as closely as possible. That way, they wouldn't have to worry about damaging their new weapons. I could always tend to their wounds with healing magic, and the company even held its own infirmary where they could be immediately treated if need be.

"Of course, I wouldn't go as far as I did when you picked that fight with me. No need to be so scared. Where's your spirit of rebellion you showed me that day? It's not like you're going to die. How can you let a defeat or two break your spirit?"

"Yes, Boss…"

"Well… In a sense, what happened the other day was inevitable. I may not look it, but I have probably been training for much longer than you think I have and had a proper teacher back in the day… Aren't you mad that you can't beat a little kid like me?!"

"W-We are!"

"Then try to kill me today!"

"Yes, Boss!"

"I can't hear you!"

"Y-Yes, Boss!"

"Good!" I turned back to Darson. "We should get going, then. Thank you for your help. Everyone?"

"Thank you!"

"R-Right. Keep up the good work, huh?"

Maybe the forced ignition of their morale was a mistake. Feeling like Darson was getting the wrong idea about me, we began to make our way out of his shop.

"Ryoma, you might have a knack for leading guys like them," Darson muttered from behind me. Did I really seem like some kind of mob boss?

■ ■ ■

When afternoon rolled around, the delinquent adventurers were sprawled all over the courtyard of the security company.

"Come on, hang in there…"

"You alive…?"

"I think so…"

The twelve of them were laid out prone and unable to move a muscle. There was nothing wrong with their skill; I just ended up pushing them to the breaking point. I always held my strikes before they landed, so no one was injured. I kept my word that they would be in better shape than they were before.

"Even when you thought you reached your limit, you still had some energy in you when you were cornered, didn't you? *Now*, you've reached your true limit, I think. It may serve you well to remember this feeling. If you end up this way on the job, the only fate that awaits you is death. An ordinary child my age could easily finish all of you off. Or a wild animal could tear into you. My point being, you need to win the battle or make your way to a safe location before you reach this state, and preferably before you're unable to perform at your best."

"Yes, Boss…" they squeaked out. They'd be just fine.

This brought me back… My dad, although he must have been going easy on me by his own definition, had never hesitated to actually hit me with his wooden sword or straight-up kick me. He would usually beat me down until I passed out too. I was an angel of a trainer compared to him.

The pile of adventurers would get in the way of the afternoon security training, so I employed the healing magic I had just learned from Maflal the other day. "Energy Charge."

33

"Huh...?!"

"How do you feel? A little better?"

"Y-Yes, Boss."

Looked like the spell was a success. I was told this spell had the effect of healing someone's stamina, but I personally thought of it as converting magical energy to physical strength. The foundation of the spell was the Heal spell and its derivatives that I had cast numerous times before. According to Maflal, while Heal spells were primarily used to close and heal wounds, they had a secondary effect of restoring the patient's stamina. Energy Charge was specialized to heal as much stamina as possible, in exchange for not healing any wounds. While it couldn't treat any injuries, it was useful for exhausted patients or as a form of life support. While healing magic was generally considered to be ineffective in treating illnesses, restoring physical stamina could aid the patient in their treatment. My particular application of the spell seemed a bit inappropriate considering its noble purpose, but these adventurers had earned a little helping hand.

Once I cast the spell on everyone, they could all stand and walk, no problem.

"Your attention, please," I called. "You shouldn't have suffered any injuries from my strikes, but you may have some scrapes and bruises from falling. Just to be safe, I would like you all to receive treatment at the infirmary. In the meantime, I'll prepare lunch. Better late than never, right? Let's meet at the dining hall after your treatments."

The group roared in excitement, like a high school football team. These delinquent newbies, after all, *were* high school age, in their late teens. I had only guessed them to be college aged because their physiques seemed well built for their years.

Having just put a dozen hungry high schoolers through the wringer, I could see they were definitely in need of a good meal. After watching them march on to the infirmary within the security company, I rushed to the kitchen. I also acquired the help of a few cooks who had shown interest in brand new recipes and the pressure cooker, so they were happy to help me out during their break.

Before we even knew it, starving boys entered the dining hall, so we quickly served them.

"Whoa!"

"That's a lot of food…"

"We can eat this?!"

"Yes. You all worked hard today, so please help yourselves."

Today's lunch consisted of bread, sausage vegetable soup, a cluster of boiled root vegetables, steamed and marinated pumpkin, and sprint rabbit stew. The bread and soup were left over from the lunch of the security employees, since I wanted to add something nutritious and filling that'd benefit young people like themselves. As for the sprint rabbit stew, I just wanted to experiment to see if I could use the pressure cooker to soften the meat.

I reiterated for them to eat as much as they wanted, and they promptly moved the contents of the pots to their dishes, and then into their stomachs. I watched, a bit taken aback by their ferocity, and they gradually began to settle at the table, starting to converse with their tablemates.

"This boiled potato…didn't we have something like this back in the village? Tastes a bit different, though."

"That's why it felt so nostalgic."

"Pumpka… We grew them on our farm too…"

"It feels too good to be true, eating this much bread. We only ever had wheat in porridge back in our village."

"Same with mine. Aren't most farming villages like that?"

"It cost too much money and energy to mill the wheat anyway. The only bread we'd make would be really hard so we could store it over the winter."

"Come to think of it, soft bread was a rare treat for going out into the city..."

"Just taste this meat. Talk about a treat. Not bad for winter."

"Right, I usually only have sausages, dried or pickled meat."

"Yeah."

"So, where are you all from?" I asked. "Do they have any specialty food or dishes?"

"Just a normal farming village. We eat a lot of wheat porridge and boiled potatoes."

"Our village, or *region*, specializes in potatoes, and we have this potato noodle. It's nothing special, though. Wheat just cost so much so we mix in powdered potatoes to bump the portions."

This piqued my interest, so I asked him to elaborate. It seemed like a dish close to some udon dishes I knew of in Japan, where they used potato starch in the noodles.

We continued eating as they told me more about dishes from their home villages, until...

"I-I can't move..."

Most of the food had disappeared from the table. I contributed, but I only ate a single serving.

"Now that was a feast."

"It's been so long since I had good food. Now I'm stuffed..."

"I haven't been this full in a while."

The boys laughed, rubbing their guts in satisfaction.

"I'm glad you enjoyed it. Can I invite you over for a meal again sometime?"

"You would?!"

I warned them that I'd probably serve them test recipes or leftovers, and they were still ecstatic. Life in the city seemed to be tough for some of them.

"It has to be a big change from your villages," I supposed.

"It sure is, Boss!"

"It felt so right when I left the village, promising to make a name for myself."

"Didn't go that easy once we made it to the city."

After having a full meal, they were more open to sharing their honest feelings with me. As I had expected, moving out of your parents' house and into the big city was a big change in any world. In the farmlands, a good portion of the population was illiterate and only traded with proper currency maybe a few times each year, almost always bartering for goods or helping each other out in the village. They were not good at dealing with or using money, even if they weren't trying to overspend. Their inexperience with money forced them to cut back on their lifestyle, and the disparity between their vision of the big city and its reality chipped away at their confidence and pride they brought with them from their village. As their attitudes started to worsen, the city folk showed them no pity. The fear of isolation in the big city brought all of these boys together. With the small comfort of their kindred spirits, they fell into the downward spiral of acting out in attempts to restore their pride only to worsen their position in the city.

"You've been kind to us, Boss."

"What makes you say that?"

"Well, you do tell us how it is, and also beat us up, but I mean…"

"He doesn't *scold* us like the people at the guild do."

"That's it! That's what I'm trying to say."

"Well… I haven't figured out life enough to tell people what to do." In a different way than these boys had, I know I had made some mistakes. "And you've already been told what's acceptable and not, haven't you? From the guildmaster, for example."

"Well, yeah."

"Then there's nothing more I can add. I'm sure all you know what you did wrong and have remorse for it deep down."

Despite their troublemaking, they were pretty straightforward. When I asked if they knew what they did wrong, all of them tried to avoid my eyes and kept quiet. That was enough to tell me that they did have remorse. Those who really didn't know what they did wrong would have given me surprised looks like they couldn't comprehend what I said, or fake a remorseful look while believing wholeheartedly that they had done nothing wrong. I was never too good at reading people, but I had worked with the unremorseful for years in my previous life. Something told me that these boys were not the type. Their wounded pride drove them to make trouble, but they knew they were misbehaving, and felt bad for it. Compared to the team I had to work with on Earth, they were much more likable.

"If you try to cause trouble in front of me, I'll stop you. By force, if I have to. If you want advice, I'll give it to the best of my ability. But at the end of the day, you have to make decisions for yourself. 'Scolding' just doesn't sound right… Personally, I would like to see all of you make a fresh start. It can take courage to admit what you've done wrong and change your attitude, but you can still start fresh. All of you."

"Start fresh…" someone incredulously muttered. I turned to him. He must not have meant for me to hear him, but he reluctantly spoke when he saw that I noticed. "We caused so much trouble here. Do you really believe that?"

My answer was yes. "You won't mend the trust you've broken right away, and even when you clean up your acts, people will treat you harshly at first. But as long as you keep it up... People who can't start over are people who feel no remorse for hurting people. I don't know if it's in their nature, or if it's nurtured through the force of habit. As long as you feel sorry for the things you have done, you can still start again."

Of course, the best choice would have been to never do these things in the first place, but changing their behavior now was much better than letting it continue on that spiral. A thoughtful silence filled the dining room. Once their stomachs had settled, the boys told me they were going home.

I walked them out to the front gate of the security company. "Be careful walking home. And even though you've been healed with magic, your bodies have gone through a lot. Get some good rest. I'll see you at work."

"Yes, Boss!"

"Thank you for our weapons, food, and training, Boss!"

"Thank you, Boss!"

I chuckled. "Just so we're clear, don't you dare use those weapons to commit crime. If you do..." I would feel some responsibility as the one who bought them those weapons. If they were to injure or kill an innocent person with those weapons... "The least I could do in recompense would be to end your life with my own hands..."

"We would never!"

"I'm kidding. You wouldn't do that, I trust you guys."

"Y-You were joking?"

"That was brutal..."

"It didn't sound like he was joking..."

With a chuckle, I waved the boys off.

"I guess I should go to church." Things had gotten so busy since my initial return to Gimul that I hadn't seen them in a while. It was time. "What should I start with... There's so much to talk about..." Musing out loud, I made my way to the familiar church.

～ Chapter 7 Episode 24 ～
Serelipta's Punishment and Ryoma's Calling

"Oh?"

After coming to the church, praying in the chapel, and opening my eyes upon sensing that I had been beamed up to the divine realm, I found all nine of the gods before me. Usually, I would be greeted by two or three on a good day. I wondered if something had happened.

"Hello, welcome."

"Wilieris, Grimp. Thanks for helping out the other day."

"T'warn't nuthin,' b'y."

"Even we couldn't condone what Serelipta did the other day. All of us congregated, and made sure to administer appropriate punishment."

"Oh… That's why you're all here. I see Serelipta's here too…"

I wasn't sure what to say or if I should have dared until this point, but Serelipta was sprawled out on the pearly white ground, if one could call it that, of the divine realm.

"Help me, Ryoma…" he said, apparently conscious but immobile.

Just as I was wondering what punishment he had faced, Wilieris groaned. "Don't pay him or his dramatics any mind."

"Is he all right?"

Fernobelia, the god of magic, answered me. "Serelipta's punishment is the temporary confinement of his powers. We left him with the bare minimum to manage his share of the world and took away the rest. That doesn't make him ill or in pain, though. He's only flopped out like a worm because he's weak… The first time you two met, you were in a giant sphere of water, right?"

"Yes, we were."

"He always kept that ball of water around him before we cut off his powers. It was an environment that gave him the most comfort and power as the god of water. A sort of barrier. While the water creates a powerful effect even from the perspective of us gods, he can't achieve his full potential without it."

"Ah." Invincibility with a clause.

"You could put it like that. Some of us didn't think curbing his powers was enough of a punishment. So, we decided to keep him weakened and put him through the same military training the 'elite warriors' go through in the human realm. Chalked up all the pain from the training regime as part of his punishment. He's just sore from head to toe. Unlike humans, physical training has absolutely no benefit for us."

Such rigorous training, knowing there's nothing to gain from it… I certainly wouldn't have wanted to do that, and Serelipta was not physically strong, to say the least.

"When Serelipta first left his ball of water, he cried uncle after walking on his feet for three minutes."

"Aren't you a bit too frail?" I turned to Serelipta.

"I don't need to walk in water, and I can go anywhere by controlling the current. Without buoyancy, my body feels so heavy… Who's the moron that invented gravity, anyway?"

The other gods glared at him, especially Gain. "Ryoma," he said. "He's well enough to complain, so no need to concern yourself with his well-being. And *I'm* the one who made gravity, by the way. I am right here, Serelipta."

"Help...me...Ryoma..." The god in question came dramatically crawling up.

"What do you expect me to do about the rules of the gods?" I asked.

"Well... You could testify or something, you know, as the, quote, unquote, '*victim*.'"

"I'm not exactly hung up over it or anything..."

"Ryoma, that groveling worm may technically be a god, but that doesn't mean you need to try and appease him."

"I'm not appeasing him, Wilieris. I did feel unsafe at the time, but I felt more sick and confused than angry. Like he said, I don't think he wanted to kill me. Looking back on it, if Serelipta wanted me dead, there wouldn't have been a thing I could have done. I came out all right, and if he already served a punishment you guys thought was fair, I don't want to demand any more."

"You really mean it."

"Well, I did lose a lot of respect for him."

I didn't think Serelipta even had ill intent, knowing the kind of god he was. The road to hell is paved with good intentions, as they say. I'd made plenty of mistakes in my previous life; there were times when I meant well but ended up causing more trouble for others, and vice versa. No sense dwelling on it.

"Hm-hmm! I knew it! You really are the best!"

"That smug attitude of yours makes it *really* dubious that you're feeling any remorse!"

"Calm down, Wilieris."

"Ryoma's got a point. I don't wanna put wind in his sails any more 'n the rest o' ya's, but lettin' 'im git under our skin ain't gonna do us any good."

"Grimp, Tekun... Understood. I was the one who asked, and Ryoma declared our handling sufficient. Let's drop the subject."

I wondered if Serelipta and Wilieris were as incompatible as they seemed, or if they only bickered from the eons they'd spent together. In any case, Wilieris had plenty to say about it. With the council of two gods and out of respect for my input, Wilieris seemed to back down.

Serelipta, meanwhile, was clinging onto me with a smile as if to say, *Don't worry, Ryoma. Since you smoothed things over, I'll keep my mouth shut for now.* He looked so feminine that I had to remind myself he was a male god.

"Get off!"

"Wait, let me lean on you, please. I really can't stand up."

He did feel weak enough that I could easily push him off if I wanted to. That made me think of fish that live deep under the sea. Apparently, they have very few bones because softer tissue can withstand the water pressure better. An angler fish, for example... I couldn't quite put my finger on it...

"What am I, a blobfish?!" Serelipta protested, but I thought "fish out of water" would be an accurate description. Just as that thought crossed my mind, the rest of the gods burst out laughing. Apparently, they had been reading my mind.

"My apologies," Gain said. "We wanted to know your honest feelings when it came to Serelipta."

"I don't mind. You know you can all read my thoughts." Knowing I couldn't lie to them had always allowed me to be honest with the gods. With their permission, I had stopped being formal with my language, even. I felt like I could talk to them naturally, without the fear of being misunderstood. It would depend on the person, of course, but having someone read your mind could certainly have its benefits... I felt like I'd thought about this before. Déjà vu, perhaps?

"That would make things easier."

"Then, let's wrap this up. I want to hear from you, Ryoma," Lulutia said, breaking her silence for the first time since I arrived.

With a clap of his hands, Kufo summoned a large and expensive-looking wooden table, aligned with enough floor chairs for everyone. Once everyone was seated, I began explaining what happened after I returned to Gimul.

"You're handling those delinquent adventurers well."

"They're calling you Boss and everything."

As it turned out, the gods were also interested in the new dynamic I had with them.

"I wish they wouldn't... I'm not *that* old. Heck, I'm not old at all."

"Why not? They're not making fun of you. It just means you have enough guts and strength that they can rely on you."

"I'm happy if they see me as someone they can trust... But in my last life, I was often mistaken for someone in *that line of work*. I've been questioned on the street and whatnot by the police, so I still have a bit of a bad taste in my mouth about it..."

"I get it. But that might be your calling," Kiriluel said.

"Really?"

I suppose anything would sound more believable coming from a god's lips. When I looked around me for confirmation—or maybe just denial—the gods just chuckled. *What the hell's that all about?*

"Any managerial position requires skill or experience. No matter what your role as an adventurer is, you gotta be able to hold your own in combat."

"And you're a caring person, Ryoma. It means a lot that you can take care of people so naturally."

"Your experience as a boss in your previous life is serving you well, however you felt about your position. Making mistakes is an important way to gain experience, and that makes a big difference."

I had to agree with Tekun, Lulutia, and Gain.

"I think you'll do even better with people working for you who have leadership and charisma. Caring as you are, those aren't your strong suits," Serelipta said, his face flat on the table.

I had to agree with that too. I had a system working exactly like that. Carme was running the laundry shop for me, and my other departments were delegated to other people who knew what they were doing, many of them sent from the duke. My job had gotten incredibly easier, leaving me plenty of time for studies and experimentation. Compared to my career on Earth, things were going unbelievably well. The results showed how I thought that this style far better suited me. At the very least, I should have had a much healthier work—life balance.

"You should have picked a better career in your previous life. Even if you couldn't be your own boss, things might have turned out differently if you chose a job that needed your caring nature. Like a school teacher."

"Some of my old coworkers told me that." Like I should have been a PE teacher, or in charge of student conduct. Either way, they had pictured me with the stereotypical look of wearing a tracksuit and carrying a bamboo sword. The conversation always ended with them teasing me that I'd be a great principal for a kindergarten, based on a character in the popular anime.

"You'd be good at taking care of kids too."

"Get out of my memories. How do you know all this?"

"Unlike the other gods, I always look into your mind when we're talking. And I read deep into your soul one time, remember?

I'm aware of most things you know. It's *me*, Ryoma, what did you expect?"

I felt a flash of rage at his brazenness, but I ignored him to not give him the satisfaction.

"In any case, I figured out that a job with more responsibility and freedom is best suited for me."

The gods all agreed. I would carry the gods' advice with me as I continue with my work.

∽ Chapter 7 Episode 25 ∽
Dealing with Snow, and
a New Branch of Slime Research

I continued my relaxed conversation with the gods, and the topic shifted from talking about farming to the weather when I was told that the winter was going to be much colder and bring more snow.

"A cold winter?"

"Actually, this is closer to normal. Do you remember why you were sent to this world, Ryoma?"

"To bring some magical energy over from Earth, right?"

"Right. All of that magic that came with you is invigorating the entire world. It's like a malnourished person getting a good meal," Kufo said.

"The climate is ever changing, anyway. Always keeping balance with various elements. The seasons will just be a bit more articulated," Fernobelia added.

It sounded like the increased cold and snow was a good thing for the world, albeit with a *bit* of climate change. Considering that's coming from the gods, us humans would have to prepare well for the winter.

"I guess it could be serious for humans."

"It shouldn't be an immediate issue as long as you've prepped for winter at all, but you can never be too careful."

Kiriluel and Lulutia confirmed my concerns.

"I've been meaning to say this, but there's some gaps or discrepancies in the knowledge you gave me on my way into this world," I said, and the three gods who had guided me across the worlds gave me an apologetic look. "I don't blame you guys for it. It's all worked out, and it was the catalyst for me getting to know everyone at the duke's."

Even humans have different knowledge and outlooks depending on their culture or generation. Of course, the gods would see the world differently than humans did.

"Thanks for understanding," said Gain.

"The passage of time can be rather fuzzy when you've been around as long as we have."

"It's hard for us to keep track of centuries, let alone decades."

Of course, that was a feeling I could never understand... As I realized that there would be more snow than usual, I was beginning to plan how to prepare for it and even create more jobs out of this.

Serelipta grinned. "Another new venture?"

"I'll start with prepping the city for snow, I think. Even if it only snows a little at a time, it could jam foot traffic if it piles up without melting. I could handle areas around my businesses with my slimes and magic, but I can't cover the entire city like that. Besides, if we're going to get heavy snow every year, it's best to start setting up for it now."

"What did you have in mind?"

"I'll start by getting all hands on deck. There are still more workers coming in. I'll prototype some shovels and other tools from Earth that can work with the snow and ice... I have a few things in mind from my slime research too..."

"Oh? And you're not dying to tell us about it? You're usually so excited about anything that has to do with slimes," Wilieris said.

Apparently, the gods would agree with my human acquaintances when it came to my excitement about slimes.

"It looks useful for getting rid of snow, but it has to be handled with care."

"Handled with care? What did you make, a bomb?" Kufo was clearly joking, but he wasn't far off the mark there. "Wait, did you really?"

"No, no. Not a bomb. I *just happened* to make something that resembled gunpowder during my experiments."

"How did we not know about this?"

"Because I haven't told you before?" There were so many other topics to discuss. "I'll explain if you want to hear," I offered.

"I do…"

"Ryoma, you already have the look in your eye," Tekun pointed out.

"I'll keep it quick, then." It all started with the acidic cleaner I had made during the hot springs cleaning job in Fatoma, which I had created by mixing the excretion of the acid and sticky slimes. While that seemed like a simple process to me, I realized that I had never tried mixing what the other slimes produced. With so many different slimes to evolve and plenty of ways to utilize them on their own, it had never crossed my mind. Looking back on it, I wished I would have experimented with them a lot sooner…but didn't mention it to the gods since that was just my personal feeling. When I first created the acidic cleaner, I found a trace amount of powder at the bottom of the solution.

I produced a vial from the Item Box and placed it on the table. "And this is a sample of that powder."

"Oh?"

"Hm."

The gods seemed to recognize what it was immediately. When I ran Appraisal on it, I got…

Super Water-Repellent Powder (Tentative)

A byproduct of mixing the acid of an acidic slime and the sticky solution of a sticky slime. A highly water-resistant powder. Flammable. Handle with care. Contains the magical energy of the slimes.

Personally, I attributed the water-repelling properties of the sticky solution to this material.

"This came from mixing the excretion of slimes?"

"The magic contained in each material had a reaction when they were mixed."

The powder certainly piqued the interest of the god of technology Tekun and the goddess of academia Fernobelia. Judging by their reaction...

"Not to sidetrack, but is this something even the gods don't see often?"

"It's not that... Well, I guess we don't usually see it in a form like this."

"It would certainly be a rare material for humans..." Gain said. "I will tell you that it's a similar material to magic stones and magic potions. It would take too long for me to explain anything more."

This powder was looking to be something a lot more complex than I had thought. "I'll take my time researching it."

"I appreciate that motivation, as the goddess of academia. Keep it up."

"Getting back on track... This powder made me curious about what could come of mixing the secretions of other slimes, so I tried them out."

"What else would you do?"

"I can just picture you having so much fun experimenting."

Kufo and Lulutia seemed to share my sentiment, but I hadn't shown them my result yet. I produced the product.

51

It was a black powder that looked like ground charcoal, but it had no sheen. The powder was made from the fertilizer of a scavenger slime and the deodorant slime's odor-absorbing solution.

"Well, it was kind of tricky. At first I was mixing them outside, in case it made any poisonous fumes, when it suddenly boiled over and exploded. Wound up burning just about everything it splattered onto. I did manage to put it out quickly, though. Basically, it's a bit like a Molotov—er, an incendiary bomb, that is. A weapon designed to burn as much surface area as possible. Gave me a heck of a shock, that's for sure."

"I'm surprised you can laugh about it, Ryoma…"

"So am I. Glad you weren't hurt."

"I had shields and an evacuation area ready for such emergencies."

Nothing ventured, nothing gained, as they say. I didn't have to worry as long as I took all the necessary safety precautions.

"Anyway, I kept researching the powder, and discovered that it can efficiently absorb light to release heat."

I had experimented by dissolving the powder in a glass of water and putting it in the light. The result varied depending on the light source, but the solution started boiling and steaming after anywhere from a few seconds to a minute in sunlight. Within three minutes, all the water evaporated and the powder itself ignited.

"It produces a decent amount of heat just from sitting in the light, so I think I can figure out a way to use this on the snow."

Scattering the powder on the snow would be enough to melt the snow, but that might lead to fires once the snow melted and eventually evaporated. It would be much safer to use the standard ground charcoal, which should produce decent results safely if combined with magic. This new powder, however, could be a game changer as long as I made sure it was safe.

"Any ideas on those safety measures?" Lulutia asked.

"Yes. You'll have some time if you just want to figure it out by the end of the season," Wilieris added, "but you won't have much time if you want it to be ready the next snow day."

"I do have an idea to prevent fires. In my previous life, especially when I was a kid, these things called incandescent bulbs were very common."

Incandescent bulbs emit light (and heat) by conducting electricity through a filament. The earliest models of the light bulb used charred paper, although by the time they were mass-produced, charred bamboo was used instead. The electrified filament produced light and heat. The question was, why didn't the filament burn in the bulb? Because it was in a vacuum. Fire required a combination of fuel, heat, and oxygen to burn. By creating a vacuum inside the light bulb, it cuts off oxygen from the filament. As a result, the electricity only caused the filament to emit light and heat without burning.

"I see, so you're going to cut off its oxygen. Any idea of what you'll use to do that?"

"The sticky slimes' hardening solution. It resists heat and is clear, so I'm thinking of mixing the powder into it. I already discovered that the black powder won't emit heat in a lightless environment created by Dark magic, so mixing it should be possible. I'm just concerned that the powder will change its properties when it's mixed into a secretion of sticky slime."

"I don't think that will be a problem. The water-repellent powder seems very stable in powder form. I expect that the black powder is stable as well. If you're just going to stir it in, it shouldn't change or react at all. The same can't be said about the *other stuff* we know well... Cool."

While I didn't know what Tekun meant by "other stuff," he was curiously peering into the water-repellent powder from every direction.

"You want to take it?" I offered. "I can make some more when I get home, so I don't mind." Tekun had given me a sake cup before. Not that I considered this an equal exchange, but...

"Oh, yeah? I'll take you up on that." Just as Tekun said so, the vial vanished from his hand. Glad to see him excited about it.

"That reminds me."

"You got another thing up your sleeve?"

"The black powder is the one that looks useful for the snow, but the other one... The one that's like a bomb like Kufo joked, or gunpowder."

"This black powder isn't that...?"

"I mean, this one does *look* like gunpowder." It would be hard to use since it's light sensitive... Wait a minute. Since it caught on fire when the light hit it, could I make a bomb triggered by light? As long as I could prevent misfires, it could work like a time bomb to—

"Your mind's wandering to bomb-making, Ryoma. Explain this other material."

"Oh, sorry, Kufo. I mixed the acid slime's acid and a fluff slime's fluff to make a cotton-like material that burns fast and bright." It reminded me of flash cotton (nitrocellulose) which I had used once on Earth when I performed a magic trick at a work party. "Nitrocellulose is also called single-base propellant based on how it's treated. I heard that's what they use in bullets."

"So it's exactly gunpowder... Except it's cotton."

"And that would be very cheap to make, wouldn't it?"

"My slimes give me plenty of material. Easy to make. To be honest, it's extremely cost effective."

"It's not uncommon for travelers from Earth to seek out guns. Many gave up in the process of figuring out the process and cost of manufacturing gunpowder... I never expected you to come across it like this."

"It was purely accidental. Besides, I'm not really into firearms, so I wouldn't know what to do with much gunpowder."

"Really?"

"Tabuchi, a coworker I got along with, knew a lot about weapons... He told me all that stuff about flash cotton. He's told me a bunch of things, but I don't have comprehensive knowledge. The firearm I'm most familiar with is the revolver, but that's just because a few anime characters I liked used them. I'm clueless about the latest firearms."

I had fired a gun a few times back when I went on a lot of business trips overseas. It never clicked with me, though, so it didn't strike my interest beyond trying it for the sake of it. I *could* use one, but it didn't sit right in my hand. Like it almost felt empty. I much preferred a bow and arrow if I were to choose a ranged weapon.

"Weapons I could reasonably make might be...flaming arrows, dynamite, and a musket? Even then, I only have some basic knowledge of them. I have no experience using any of them, let alone making them. Personally, I'm more interested in peaceful applications like mining or demolition. I wouldn't mind researching firearms when I have the time... But if I do, I would keep it a secret except from Reinhart and his people. I'd actually let them deal with it entirely."

"That would be wise," Gain assured, followed by Kufo and Lulutia.

I felt like Reinhart's woeful expression flashed before my eyes... Weird.

∽ Chapter 7 Episode 26 ∽
The Pros and Cons of Slime Magic

"I'm accumulating more and more secrets as I continue researching my slimes." On the other hand, it meant that my research was valuable and useful. And not that anything could be dangerous if misused.

"Speaking of secrets." Kiriluel turned to Fernobelia. "Didn't you have something to discuss with Ryoma?"

"You do?"

"Remember how you used sand magic the other day by combining familiar magic with the Synchronize ability of the slime? There's a few things I wanted to go over with you."

"You know, it's really rare to see Fernobelia join in the fun like this, even though we had Serelipta's thing to deal with," Kiriluel added.

Fernobelia had something that important to discuss?! If I had known, I would have held off all of my ramblings about my slimes.

"It's all right. I appreciate your enthusiasm for studying topics of your interest. Sharing your findings is also an important aspect of academia."

"Thank you."

I wondered what was there to discuss about my technique? Could it be...

"Before you get your hopes down, I won't tell you not to use it. There are a few things you should be careful of, but I encourage you to use it as often as possible. Kufo mentioned the reason why you came to this world. I won't go into detail, but after examining your new technique on our end, we found there's a chance it improves the magical energy of this world."

What?!

"While the effect is indirect and minuscule," Fernobelia continued, "many a mickle makes a muckle, as humans would put it. The accumulation of small efforts is sometimes needed to solve a great problem. We can't afford to overlook any influence in the right direction."

I never would have expected that spell to have such a side effect. On a personal level, I used magical energy when I cast spells. But that increased the magical energy on a world level.

"If it piques your interest, you should study it. It only produces this result because of the slimes' involvement in it."

"Really?"

Fernobelia affirmed. It didn't seem like he wanted to withhold information from me but left me room to do my own research and let me continue my hobby of researching slimes. As the god of academia, he must prefer humans to reach their own conclusions, if it can be helped.

"There are three points you must be careful of. Its effect, its uniqueness, and the effect it has on your slimes. As you must have already noticed, your technique allows you to cast more powerful magic and have greater control over it. Combining your large stock of magical energy and a great number of slimes, it has the potential to yield similar results to the calamity magic that once threatened this world."

"Calamity magic... I've never heard of that before, but it sounds less than peaceful."

"It was just a combination of ordinary, elemental spells. The one who wielded those spells, however, was another traveler from Earth, an ancestor of the duke you've befriended."

"The one who specialized in magic?"

"That's the one. He created powerful magic with his scientific knowledge and fired it off as he was told, causing massive casualties. It was wartime, after all. Eventually, it came to be called calamity magic out of fear and respect. We considered it impossible for a spell like that to be created again. Certainly not by anyone native to this world, and not even by a traveler unless they also specialized in magic. With you and your slimes, however, I see a possibility of it in your future. It would be helpful for us if you used the spell often, but be careful of the time and place, and your execution. Nothing bigger than the demolition projects you've been using them for."

"Thank you for letting me know."

Fernobelia nodded and continued, "It's unique because, more than being a skilled spellcaster, you need clear communication and great compatibility with the slime through familiar magic to make this technique work. Without them, the spell may not be effective or it may even misfire. It's easy for you and your high compatibility with slimes, Ryoma, but it would be difficult to learn or practically impossible for most others. Like many of your other discoveries, be careful who you pull back the curtains for."

"Understood." What I was most curious about was the effect on my slimes.

"The more you use that technique, the more the synchronization skill of your slime will level up. Once it's at level 10, the slime will become the element it synchronized with and return to nature."

"You mean...they'll die?"

"We don't see it that way. But it is death in the sense that humans are used to. You will lose that familiar."

This was the worst. In exchange for great power, I would be shortening the life span of my slimes. Everything else, I just had to be careful about sharing my secrets and keeping the effect of the spell contained. Since the spell was improving the magical energy in the world as a whole, I was secretly ready to fire it off every chance I got. But now...

"I do encourage you to use it often, but it will always be your choice."

"Thank you."

There was no question as to which was more important—it was my feelings and the lives of a few slimes versus the entire world. The gods had the power to force me if they wanted to, so I appreciated them respecting my free will on this.

At this point, I noticed that the other gods were giving Fernobelia and me the stink eye.

"What's wrong?" I asked.

"It's fine if Ryoma's good with it, but you'll have to give him more than that, Fernobelia," said Kiriluel.

"You're making things awkward by cherry-picking information," Tekun joined.

"I understand why you omitted explaining it," Wilieris said, "and so does Ryoma, but..."

Even Serelipta chimed in, "You're very kind, Ryoma. Not that I haven't benefited from that, but you could demand a better explanation."

"Fernobelia isn't lying," Gain finally said. "But using that spell a few times won't kill your slime. It's not that dire of an issue."

"Right. The lack of magical energy is something we have to deal with. If you don't want to use that spell, that's completely okay," Lulutia said.

"Most importantly," Kufo chimed in, "do you remember how your slime was after using that technique."

Come to think of it, I had started using that spell as a game. It seemed like the slimes enjoyed it too. "It has a positive effect on the slimes as well?"

"Yes. At the very least, that spell won't cause the slime any pain. Fernobelia said so too."

I turned to Fernobelia, and he gave a nod, his stoic expression shaded with the slightest hint of guilt.

"You didn't want to rob Ryoma of the joy of discovery by giving him too much information. I understand that, but you leaned a little too heavy into the demerits," Gain said.

In that case, I would put a pin in this issue. I would make sure to use that spell only when needed, keeping a close eye on the synchronization skill of the slimes. I would continue researching slimes to uncover the details Fernobelia was keeping from me... No matter how many decades it would take. I shared my nonspecific direction with the gods.

"That's the spirit, b'y," Grimp said. "Ye gots plenty o' time."

"Fernobelia..." Serelipta squeezed out before laughter overtook him.

"Your point, Serelipta?" Fernobelia grunted.

"I've never seen you be considerate before. And you like Ryoma so much that you want him to be franker with you, but you just can't bring yourself to say so? You know, they call your type 'tsundere' in Japan?"

"What does that even mean? I simply appreciate the attitude to study the powers given to one instead of using them as they're told. Ryoma isn't the first to do so. The other traveler, his application of the calamity magic notwithstanding, applied effort and creativity to his spellcraft. I *can* give fair praise when it's deserved..."

"I hear tsundere's more of a *girl* thing, though."

"Won't you ever listen?!" Fernobelia shouted at Serelipta, but he just laughed it off.

"It's refreshing to see how not only Fernobelia, but everyone else, treats you. They all act a bit differently with you."

Serelipta's comment seemed to give the others some pause. I wondered if I dared ask.

"Of course you can ask." Serelipta grinned, still facedown on the ground. "It's all relevant to you. Heck, it's *all* about you."

What's he on about?

"Didn't you know? Normally, living humans can't visit the divine realm like you can. Travelers aren't usually an exception to that. The only way for almost all humans to hear us is the Oracle skill that only a select few who devote their lives to the church have. Even then, they can only hear what we have to say."

I had heard his explanation before; I was certainly different, even by traveler standards.

"Yes," Serelipta continued. "Although we have to summon you first, you can come up here in spirit form to speak to us face to face. No one in this world had done that before. None of us have much experience talking to people like this. We don't need to talk with each other when we can just send what we're thinking from afar. That's why we rarely experience a misunderstanding like the one that happened between you and Fernobelia just now. The Oracle skill is usually a one-way path from god to person, by the way."

"I see... So back when I first came here, that was just a basic rundown you gave me..."

"I'm sure it's partly due to the difference in how we see the world, but it must have also been because we didn't know how to convey that information. There are so many things that seem obvious to us, but not to you. It's so fun to watch them trying to account for that when they communicate with you."

I wondered what Serelipta thought of the subject.

"Me? I may be a bit different from my normal self… But I treat everyone equally. Do you think I'd ever be *considerate* with anyone, god or mortal?"

"Man, I really feel like I wasted my breath," I said. Not a chance that he ever felt a shred of consideration for anyone. The rest of the gods seemed to share my sentiment.

"Aw, you meanie," Serelipta whined. "Can't we still be friends?"

"All right, all right, just get off me! You're…well, not that heavy, I suppose, but still, just get off!" Though he was bizarrely lightweight, it was still a pain in the ass having him clinging to my leg.

"It doesn't feel right that Serelipta pointed it out, but I suppose we might be acting a bit differently than our usual selves," Gain said.

"I agree. Come to think of it, we didn't gather often before Ryoma came along. I can't remember the last time all nine of us were together."

"We used to meet up when this world was new."

"Civilization was still small back then. The world kept on expanding and progressing."

"We started doing our own things since we could always send each other all the information we need."

"Even when we got together, not everyone needed to show up."

"Upon self-reflection, we only met out of necessity."

"Even when we met up, we never used to just talk over some drinks."

Maybe this was akin to working from home for too long. Not that I wanted to conflate their divine powers with the technology on Earth…

"It's very similar," Gain answered. "In our case, we may not see each other for centuries, or even millennia. Especially *one of us* who I can't even remember when we last saw… We need to show a bit of gratitude for Ryoma giving us more opportunities to meet."

"I didn't do anything myself, but that's good to hear." If they were happy, then so was I. "Was there anything else I wanted to talk about…?" I could talk about slimes for hours, but… "Anything else important? Like, well, you know."

"Well, we won't 'ave to warn ya's too often. I gots plenty to tell ya's about farmin' an' all, but no sense droppin' all that on ya before ya come round on what we're discussin' now. That's all the input I got fer today, so…" Grimp gestured to the rest of the gods.

"I'll start," the voice by my foot said.

"Go on…"

"No need to be so on edge. This was something I discussed with Kiriluel as well."

"With me? What is this about, Serelipta?"

"Don't you remember? We're talking about how Ryoma should train his sixth sense."

"Sixth sense? I remember you mentioning something like that during your punishment training. Thought you were just trying to buy time for a break."

So they did really discuss it beforehand. What did they mean by sixth sense?

"You're pretty brain-heavy," Kiriluel said.

"Hm? I guess so. I can't really tell."

"It's not a bad thing," she continued, "depending on the time and place. If you want to explain something, for example, you should make it logical. But sometimes, you just need to take action without working out the logic."

I agreed, and she further clarified that, while it varied from person to person, there should be a healthy balance between logic and impulse, and I was leaning too heavily into the logic side.

"Serelipta and I agreed that you're actually more inclined towards impulse, like a sixth sense."

"Really?"

"Mm-hm. I think your previous life might have conditioned you to be more logical in your thinking," Serelipta said. "Many people experienced in their craft in this world might rely on their experience or intuition, but logic and data are given more weight on Earth where technology is more advanced. You had no choice but to build a logical thought process in a world like that. Your aversion to interpersonal communication might have made you practice your logical thinking more. In exchange, you can't take full advantage of your talent."

"You say that…"

"Remember how you said you messed up the other day?"

"Yeah. When the air in the city and the meeting hall reminded me of how my office felt on Earth."

"That's it. If you had been able to grasp that *feeling* accurately, you might not have gone rogue."

"I just had a bad feeling. I—"

"Can't explain it?" Serelipta dramatically pulled himself up to give me a *you just don't get it, do you?* look.

I wasn't going to give him the satisfaction. Stay calm. "I don't get it. Explain."

"Oh, all right… 'Intuition' and 'sixth sense' might sound a bit vague, but I'm not just blowing smoke here. Humans learn and adapt. Most mortal creatures do, of course. Let's say there's a dog and its owner. The owner beats the dog with a stick, day after day without reason. How will the dog start to act around its owner?"

Cower or run from its owner, or show animosity and fight back... Something like that. The dog would stop showing affection, at any rate.

"Why's that?" Serelipta asked.

"Getting beaten hurts, and it might get hurt. Why would the dog want that for itself?"

"Exactly. The dog learns that getting beaten with a stick hurts, and that its owner is the one causing it pain. Like Ryoma said, the dog will then try to get away from the source of its pain or try to get rid of it. Either way, it will act to avoid any danger to its well-being. That's self-preservation. An instinct that any creature has. And even artisans treasure experience and instinct built from it. Right, Tekun?"

"You could say so. The best blacksmiths adjust their work based on the change in temperature and moisture in the air, on top of the furnace temperature or the color of the fire. Conscious or not, muscle memory can be pretty handy."

"And Ryoma carries his memories and experiences from his previous life. *Now* you get it, don't you?" Serelipta said, and collapsed onto the table.

Now that I thought about it, I acted just like the beaten dog. I felt danger, and tried to eliminate the cause of it. Plus, I could see the merit in Tekun's insight. "Serelipta..."

"Yes?"

"I didn't think you were so observant about people..."

"That's your takeaway?! I'm a god, you know!" His pompous grin faded in a flash.

"Well, you just seemed like such a self-centered god on our first encounter. I'm more surprised than anything."

"Huuuuuuh?"

"But I think I understand what you're saying."

"That's fine, then... Pain and fear are forms of experience in themselves. People call it trauma if it binds and hurts you, but it can also be made into a powerful tool. I think you should work on your intuition, Ryoma. No matter how you handled it, you were able to read the room. You have an inclination for it."

"All right, I'll keep that in mind," I said, just as my surroundings began to glow.

"Good timing," Gain said.

"I forgot we had a time limit. I feel like we talked more than usual, though."

"All nine of us called you this time."

"Apparently, you can stay longer the more of us there are."

"It's a good excuse for us to get together. We should do this more often."

"Are you going straight home after this, Ryoma?" Serelipta asked out of nowhere.

"After I'm back at the church? I think I will. I don't have any more plans, so I might go home and look into that spell and the synchronizing slimes... Oh."

"You do have something?"

"I wasn't planning on it, but I might stop by the orphanage."

"The one you rebuilt?"

"Right. I asked the kids there to do a little job for me. I'm sure they're doing fine, but I want to check in on them."

"Sure, why not?" Serelipta responded as if he hadn't just asked. On second thought, it was more like...

"Three nights before the end of the year..."

"Huh?"

"Be at the abandoned mines alone. You might find your way."

"You're—"

It became brighter around me, signaling the time for my return.

"Buh-bye!"

"Time's up."

"See you next time!"

On Serelipta's lead, everyone bid me farewell as the light swallowed me whole... And I returned to the familiar chapel.

Three nights before the end of the year, be at the abandoned mines alone. You might find your way. Apparently, Serelipta was waiting for a moment to slip me a message without the other gods noticing. I didn't know what way I was supposed to find, or what Serelipta wanted out of it, but one thing was clear: Serelipta was scheming something again... He never learned his lesson, did he?

I decided it was time to go, when the sister of the church stopped me. "Excuse me, Takebayashi, sir. Can I have a moment of your time?"

"Oh, yes. No problem. What is it?"

"It's about that soup kitchen you offered to help us with..."

⤳ Chapter 7 Episode 27 ⤳
Ryoma the Medical Intern

"Right, slimes are taken care of, research plans look good, the goblins are fed, and I've taken a bath. Now then…"

Late that night, I decided to use what time I had before bed to ponder my spellcasting with the slimes. Inspiration struck, and I called over a mud slime that was looking bored near the puddle in the corner. Then I cast Sensory Sharing, a Tamer spell mainly used for reconnaissance. Sharing another's sight was the most common use case for this spell, but it also allowed for the sharing of the other senses. With slimes, however, the spell had no effect, since they lacked sensory organs, or so I'd heard at Reinhart's when I learned about the spell.

Sure enough, I could feel nothing through my usual five senses, but I was counting on my sixth sense—magic detection, which was a prerequisite to learn and use this spell. Every magic user could detect magical energy, though accuracy varied. It was no mere placebo, but a tangible sensation. I had also noticed through my experience experimenting with slimes that magic played a large part in everything from hypothesizing to theorizing and testing. That's why I decided to try sharing magic detection.

I felt a faint resistance, and then, **BAM**! The sudden glut of information that came flooding in almost knocked me off my feet. I couldn't decipher what bits of information there were; I could only suck in the torrent of data. Suddenly, I started to feel feverish, dizzy, and nauseous all at once, topped off with a severe headache. I felt burned out, not unlike how I'd been accustomed to feeling at the job I worked in my previous life. Of course, back then, I still had to come in even when sick. But now, there was quite literally nothing which said I had to take all this, or feel guilty about not being able to take it. I cut off the spell, and the flood of information ceased. Relief washed over me, but there was still some lingering discomfort afterwards.

"I'll have to be more careful...and figure out what's happening."

■　■　■

I felt better the next morning. I planned to work and study at the hospital that day, so I jumped to the city with space magic and walked the rest of the way to the hospital. After changing into my lab coat in the locker room, I reported to the hospital wing break room, where Maflal and his five apprentices from the duke's were already congregating.

"Good morning!"

"Morning. Once more unto the breach, eh?"

After the morning meeting, we went over our work for the day. After going over each of our tasks, we were left with a little bit of time before work began. So, I decided to ask them about the symptoms I'd experienced the previous night, just to be safe during this important time. I asked them if they had any causes for similar symptoms in mind.

"Physically, you're doing just fine. Your symptoms must have been caused by mental stress and exhaustion. You overworked your brain, not your body."

"Yes. No need for any treatment, per se. Rest would be the only thing, but if you don't have any issues now, you should be able to maintain your work schedule. Your circumstances are curious, though. A vast amount of data came flooding in when you Sensory Shared with a slime... I have heard that less experienced tamers may feel sick from the mixing of their own and the familiar's senses," Maflal said, alluding to the phenomenon where a shaky video could make you sick.

I had experienced that when I first started practicing Sensation Sharing, but... "It felt different from that. It was like being forced to read mountains of documents at high speed..."

"Then I'm not sure. I have fragments of knowledge on the topic from working for the Jamils, but Taming magic is outside of my expertise."

"I have an appointment with Taylor, so I'll ask him about it then."

"Yes, that should be best."

"Could it be...? No..." Clarissa muttered.

"Any ideas?" I asked.

"It reminded me of the Magic Eyes story from my childhood."

Boom. Some fantasy-sounding thing outta nowhere.

"The Magic Eyes?"

"You haven't heard of it? It's a legend of a famous adventurer and was even made into a fairy tale... Oh! I have heard that different races and regions call it something different. Elves like Maflal, for example, should know it as Fairy Eyes."

"I'm sorry, I'm not familiar with too many fairy tales or legends."

"Oh, really?"

"You know more about medicine than me..."

"I always thought you knew about all sorts of things. I didn't expect you not to know such a famous fairy tale!"

I chuckled, since my knowledge of medicine was given to me by the gods. They'd been real lifesavers for me lately.

"Then let me give a quick summary... Magic Eyes allows its holder to see a world different from the one everyone else sees. In exchange, or when the holder is unable to utilize their eyes, the eyes are said to cause terrible migraines or consume the holder's mind."

"Interesting," I said. I could see the resemblance between the story and my situation.

"The Magic Eyes are supposed to be a powerful weapon if used properly, but the migraines afterwards are brutal."

"It's often compared to having your skull bashed in or your brain being fried!"

"Most born with Magic Eyes are said to choose their own death, most of the time..."

"That's scary."

"Yes, and I was only reminded of it. If you had it Ryoma, I don't think you would be talking to us right now."

We shared a laugh at this.

"It's about time, everyone," said Maflal. "Let's do some good work today."

"Yes!"

We each moved to our stations. I first headed to the dispensary, accompanied by Ector, the quiet expert in pharmaceuticals and especially antivenom. At the hospital wing, he was usually the one in charge of dispensing medicine for its patients. My objective was to learn from him as I assisted his work. Plus, he seemed like the researcher type. I got along and talked the most with him out of the apprentices.

"Oh, that's right, Ryoma. About the stock of medicinal herbs that we were talking about..."

Back in our morning meeting, the doctors had shown concern that this winter was going to be particularly cold, so much so that it would affect the health of our patients. Ector mentioned that he wanted to stock up on as many medicinal herbs as we could in preparation.

"If you can make a list of what you need, I'll gather as many of them as I can. Speaking of, I collected the herbs I'd left with the children yesterday."

"The children...from the house you rebuilt."

Considering how much medicine the hospital went through, we needed many ingredients and man-hours to process it. These ingredients could be just about anything; some were dangerous to handle without proper knowledge, while others could easily be processed by anybody. So, I had asked the children at the orphanage to take on the simple steps of processing the medicinal herbs for hospital use. They happily agreed. I figured it wouldn't be a bad deal for them, since I was told that they were already working whatever jobs they could to make ends meet.

"Are they ready?" asked Ector.

"I gave them a once-over last night, and they look good. Do you want to see them now?"

"Yes, please. Everything you got. I'll check them."

I produced what I picked up the previous day from my Item Box.

Ector opened each box of processed herbs and a grin spread across his face. He seemed pleased with the children's work.

"Looks good... I can tell they weren't rushed."

"Just because the work is simple, it doesn't mean everyone who works them will put the time in to do them right. I think they did a great job and I'm thinking of offering them the same work again."

"Let's begin."

"Yes."

I was used to the sudden change of subject and extended silence. After putting away the herbs, we started our work. We seldom talked while we worked, as the wrong mixture or quantity of drugs could harm a patient. We each devoted our attention to the task at hand and only spoke when we had to, only focusing on mixing the requested medicine correctly. One after another...

"Ryoma."

"Yes, what is it?"

"Let's take a break." Ector was holding two steaming cups.

"What? Oh, crap... It's been three hours already."

He had prepared us drinks, seeing that I was about to reach a break in my work.

"I just noticed myself," he said. "Usually, other people snap *me* out of my work... I've never met someone who got lost in this work more than I do. Does your drink look okay?"

"Well..."

"Right, it's your usual... I watched how much water and leaves you put in, so it should be the same ratio... I've been meaning to ask, but this tea is herbal, right? Roasted dante root, dried mogwart, and if I'm not mistaken, gilkoda leaves."

"Right on the money." He identified three ingredients of my go-to herbal tea since my previous life, dandelion coffee, just by looking at it.

"What are the benefits?"

"Dietary supplement, improved blood flow, calming, detoxing, and strengthening the stomach lining."

"The mogwart can treat all sorts of symptoms. It's called the backyard cure-all."

"Would you like to try it?" I offered.

"Well, if you're offering..."

He was staring daggers at my cup... And I knew how he felt. I would have that same look if someone had a mysterious slime with them. We silently exchanged cups, and I sipped on his tea. I would have never said this out loud since Ector made the tea for me, but I couldn't say that his cup of tea was enjoyable at all.

"Oh." Ector suddenly turned his attention from the dandelion coffee to me. "I'm impressed you can gather so many herbs in the winter."

"A few herbs became much easier to get after I started growing them. And the slimes help a lot."

"I guessed as much. I thought it would have been more realistic to use the secretion of medicine slimes. You have slimes that can grow herbs?"

"I only realized it recently, but weed slimes make it possible."

The key here was that there was technically no classification of *weed* in botany. For example, while mogwart was used medicinally, it was often found growing on empty plots in the city, and treated like a weed. In other words, "weeds" were just grasses that humans found inconvenient. The weed slimes fed on any grass on that extensive list. Instead of preferring medicinal or poisonous plants specifically, they ate anything that grew out of the ground, similar to how metal slimes ate anything metallic. Using the weed slimes' tendency to grow weed for cover, I was able to farm medicinal herbs. They hadn't grown naturally before because of my poor direction. They must have picked up on what I considered to be weeds and avoided growing any grass that I found useful. This was a good reminder for me to watch out for my preconceptions if I wanted to improve my research.

"The weed slimes only need water, sunlight, and scavenger slime fertilizer. With the trash plant, I can get lots of fertilizer every day.

If we wanted to, I could mass-farm medicinal herbs as well. I guess I've already started."

While I'd discovered that weed slimes could grow both medicinal and poisonous plants if I wanted them to, I still wanted to utilize my herb slimes and poisonous plant slimes. For the time being, I picked out candidates from the countless weed slimes that preferred wood magic and poison magic. All I had to do was wait for them to evolve.

"To tell you the truth, I was never very interested in slimes before you came... But there's much to learn about them."

"It makes me happy that you see the potential in them."

There was another discovery I had made through studying slime secretion, but I had a feeling that I would greatly exceed our break time if I mentioned it, so I'd save that topic for another time.

We soon went back to work, and I kept my head down until I was finished with my quota.

"Ector, I'm done with the work here."

"Thank you. I can take care of the rest."

"I'll get going to my next station, then."

That's what I did. My next post was examining and treating patients. The front lines. For the most part, the patients were my employees working in other sectors of the business. Most of them were laborers who had traveled far to Gimul only to struggle in the city until they started working for me. Some of the workers had gotten sick from the difference in work environment or schedule, and exhaustion caught up with others now that they could catch a breath. All of them were entitled to free treatment at the hospital wing as a form of community service and practice for me and the doctors.

"Hello."

"There you are. Perfect timing," said Maflal. The other three apprentices had already begun seeing patients in their examination rooms.

Seeing that the nurses I'd hired were frantically going in and out of the exam rooms, we had a lot of patients today.

"The security team just arrived."

"That's for me," I said. "I'll get ready now."

By the way, Maflal's training had been tailored to each apprentice's goals. For example, mine was to maintain good health so I could keep working as an adventurer, and to improve my chances of surviving worst-case scenarios. As a result, I didn't need the knowledge and technique to diagnose any symptom. That would be ideal, of course, if I could learn all of the knowledge and practice all of the techniques needed to do so. That, however, would take far too much time. A master doctor who devoted their life to medicine might achieve this by the end of their life, which I had no interest in doing. All I wanted to learn was how to maintain the health of myself and my party, how to administer first aid when needed to make sure I could keep myself and my team alive long enough to bring them to a real doctor. The most important part of accomplishing this was...

"Thank you for seeing me!"

"Ammos? I remember you came in last week too. I appreciate that you are out there protecting the people and that I get to practice my treatment on you, but aren't you pushing it a bit far?"

"Heh, my captain said the same thing. But I had to protect this kid..."

"Now you have your arm in a sling."

"I got hit by a piece of lumber."

"Any other injuries? Did you get hit in the head?"

"I kept my head guarded, sir. Got hit in the back, but no problems there."

"I'll take a look at that, just in case. Turn around, please."

My field of choice here was treating battle wounds like these. The people of the security teams who protect the people of the city with their lives were the perfect subjects for me to practice my craft on so I can learn the best spells, medicine, and equipment to use in treating these injuries. Not to mention that they were also great practice for the other apprentices. While the hospital wing did give priority to treating the members of the security team, I was grateful that they trusted a rookie like me to treat them, especially since their livelihoods depended on their health. I had to give every examination and treatment my all if I wanted to reciprocate that respect.

After examining Ammos's wounds, I determined that I could heal his back with Heal and his broken arm with High Heal.

"Your back is bruised, but it didn't affect your spine, so I can treat it with healing magic. Is that all right?"

"Yes, please, Little Doc."

The patients had somehow started calling me Little Doc. I would have preferred something like "the young doctor," but they say all of the doctors here were young. All four of the apprentices were in their twenties, and even Maflal looked the same age as them. "Little Doc" was the best nickname to designate me, I supposed.

With a green light from Maflal, I cast the Heal spell. He had given me tips on how to effectively cast healing magic as well. Before, I had simply cast the spell with a vague visualization of the trauma healing. Professional healers, however, had a few things to keep in mind. One of them was the image of the magical skeleton. Living beings had a skeleton composed of magical energy overlapping their physical skeleton. This also accounted for the source of magical energy for spellcasters, and it was a particularly important concept for casting healing spells.

According to Maflal, the magical skeleton holds information about that person's physicality. When using healing spells, one was supposed to sense the patient's magical skeleton to scan the information of their physical skeleton and visualize healing their wounds to match how their body should be...which was easier said than done. I was able to sense my patient's magical skeleton when concentrating, but only as a vaguely humanoid lump of magical energy. I was getting no information from it at all.

But, for some reason, I felt like I was making progress today. While I still couldn't extract any information, I could sense his magical skeleton much more clearly. When I focused on the bruise on his back, I felt a slight discrepancy there... Could this be what Maflal was talking about? After visualizing how the bruise would heal, I cast my spell.

"Heal."

The bruise faded away immediately, his skin restored to its original color. I had guessed that I would need to cast the spell at least twice... But my spell seemed more effective. I double-checked his back, and all seemed well.

Next, I cast High Heal on his broken arm. This time, the arm was completely healed after two instances when I had expected to need three.

"You fixed me up, all right! Thanks, Little Doc!"

"Take care."

After our patient left, Maflal smiled at me. "I see you're getting the hang of sensing magical skeletons."

"Is that what I felt?"

"I don't know what you felt, but it certainly seemed like you did. The effectiveness of healing spells changes drastically by whether or not you can obtain information from your patient's magical skeleton. The spells you cast today were much more effective than when you last showed me. But this is just the beginning. If you study the reading of magical skeletons further, you can cast a spell to mend severed limbs. If you master it, I hear you can immediately tell every ailment and injury the person has."

That would make me a human CAT scan machine.

"Of course, achieving that requires enormous effort and time. I have all the life experience of an average human, but still have not reached that stage."

"What's important is not losing what clicked for you just now. Let's bring our next patient in. Oh, preferably a patient on whom you can cast a healing spell. I'll go pick one out."

Maflal left the exam room and began sending me patient after patient who required healing spells. He was usually a very calm and intellectual mentor, but I learned today that he also had a more drill sergeant side to his teaching style.

⤙ Chapter 7 Episode 28 ⤚
Suspicious Movements and the Strategy Meeting

The intake of patients dwindled as the afternoon dragged on. The apprentice doctors took turns on outpatient duty, spending their free time for study and research, which they enthusiastically shared with each other.

Tint the athlete was interested in protein and physical training. Ector, a student of medicine and poison, searched for safer anesthetic and painkillers. Clarissa, who had shown great interest in supplements, was studying exactly that. Each of them helped me out with their specialty.

I had started exchanging results with Isabelle.

"Thanks again."

"Don't mention it; I'm interested in this stuff as well. Let's talk about that makeup remover sample again."

She was helping me out with my worst branch of research—beauty products. When I visited the Jamils in the past, I had made bath bombs and sugar scrubs, which had given Elise the wrong impression that I was skilled in making beauty products. Not that she had asked me for any, but I wanted to work on studying and developing those products as well. Isabelle, a female doctor, was a great ally for this venture.

We would receive an emergency patient once in a while, but our afternoon floated by uneventfully. Since the hospital was doing fine financially, I didn't complain about it being empty.

■ ■ ■

In the evening, just as I was getting ready to go home, Lilian the maid knocked at our door.

"Master Ryoma, a moment of your time."

I was ready to leave anyway, so we moved to the meeting room where Hughes and Jill from the security company, Zeph and Camil, who took care of the garbage plant, and Lilian, Lulunese, and Liviola from the support team were waiting for us. They were all members sent to us from the duke's, but I also spotted Lilyn from the laundry shop.

"Lilyn?"

"Good evening, sir."

Not that she wasn't welcome, but I had never seen her among the duke's staff before. I took my seat, eager to hear what they had to say.

Their leader (in training) Hughes spoke first. "Let's start, now that Ryoma's here. I'll cut to the chase. Our *research* is about eighty percent done." Ah, our *research*. What did he mean by eighty percent? "We're almost done, so we can keep going like we have been... But we noticed someone acting weird through our research. I wanted to discuss what to do with him."

"Who is it?"

"Hudom, a new security hire at the laundry shop."

Hudom...

"I assume you've been looking into him, since Lilyn's here."

"That's right," she confirmed.

"I know we're asking for forgiveness before permission, but we just wanted to double-check," said Hughes. "Right?"

"Yes. Just my intuition and my father's at first. No proof. He stepped outside a lot when he wasn't working."

"He takes care of work, and everyone wants fresh air during their break once in a while," Hughes said. "I certainly do. So it didn't seem off that he was doing that."

"But she and her father used to make their living in the underground," Jill chimed in. "They must have sensed something."

Lilyn nodded. "Something was off. So I followed him. He was happy when I told him I'd show him around town."

"Yeah... I can see that," I admitted. Hudom seemed the type to get around a bit. On the other hand, he's a very friendly security guard popular among kids and ladies who visit the shop. "I assume there's bad news."

Lilyn eyed Lulunese who held a few pieces of paper in her hand that contained notes on Hudom's actions.

"He was only walking around the city at first, but he's been prying a lot more lately. Mostly around locations that have to do with you, Master Ryoma. He came to the hospital because he 'tripped,' and asked to stand in and watch the training for the security company, according to the employees here."

"We know he went over to the plant as well. The children at the orphanage told us he's shown himself over there."

"Plus he's apparently been walking around the former slums, talking to the construction workers during their breaks."

"Rezoned or not, it's unusual to wander around the former slums without reason."

"Finally, and this happened just the other day, Master Fay saw him leave the shop looking particularly conspicuous. He followed him into an alley and saw him exchanging what appeared to be a letter with another man."

Lulunese, Camil, Zeph and Liviola provided this information. This did seem strange, especially the bit about the letter... "Lulunese, with this much evidence against him, I think it's safe to say he's a spy."

"We're positive he is. According to Lilyn, he seems too obvious for someone of that profession. Like he's untrained."

I looked to Lilyn to confirm.

"I talked with my father as well. For sure. We think he just sells information."

"I see." The truth was that I hadn't known Hudom very long. There were sure to be things I didn't know about him and things he hadn't told me. Whether he was a professional spy or not, I couldn't have him bring harm to us. That being said, he didn't seem like a person to betray us like that, even if he seemed a bit careless at times. But I wasn't exactly confident in my assessment of character anyway, now that Fay and Lilyn, who used to make a living in the underground, determined that he was a spy. There was no mistaking it.

"The question is how to deal with this," I said.

"Right. There's no doubt this Hudom's selling info to someone. No point nabbing the little guy making pocket change, though. Fay says whoever Hudom is meeting is the real deal. They're the one we have to grab. But a real spy can pick up on any small move we make and disappear. We have to be careful."

"Can we tell what our damage is... How much has he told?"

"Judging by where he's been, he most likely has sold little more than rumors that anyone could get access to with a little bit of research. He hasn't snuck into anywhere with vital secrets… That's our problem."

According to Jill, we easily caught Hudom selling information but said information wasn't harmful to us to get out. It might have even included information we had made public. This meant that, while annoying, he could let him continue his side hustle for the time being. It was so easy to catch Hudom in the act that they even suspected the info buyer was using him as bait.

"We can capture him or let him carry on, but I want to decide today," Hughes said.

The others took turns sharing their opinions, and when it was all said and done, the room split four to four on the two options when it came to my turn. All eyes were on me. I gave some consideration and told them my vote. Our meeting became a bit chaotic after that, but we did reach a conclusion.

"We will execute the plan tomorrow night. That's all."

"Make sure you're ready."

■　■　■

The next morning, I started improving the interior of the security headquarters and the hospital. I had two reasons for doing so. First, I had prioritized hiring workers and running the companies until now, putting the interior on the back burner after building it up enough for each facility to run. Now that the businesses had settled, I wanted to at least spruce up the reception area of the headquarters and the waiting room of the hospital.

So, I had placed a wooden stand I'd ordered in the middle of the expansive room that previously had held nothing but the reception desk and some chairs. Then, I placed a giant aquarium tank that I had made with the hardening solution to match the size of the stand. I had also prepared a few smaller tanks so I could divide the reception area from the waiting room.

I thanked the construction workers who had helped me out and saw them off.

"First, water magic."

After filling the tank halfway up with water, I spread dirt with synchronized mud slimes in it in the bottom of the tank. Then, I scaped the tank with aquatic weed slimes and stone slimes before releasing shell slimes to live in the tank. The most important part, however, was to have a cleaner in the tank who could maintain the water quality. I put in a filter slime and a newly evolved aqua slime.

The aqua slime evolved from a slime that preferred water magic, and had a liquid body. That was very important. It wasn't a slime that *used* water magic, but a liquid slime like the bloody slime. It only consumed water, and this individual evolved after drinking an endless amount of it. The aqua slime had the Synchronization skill like the mud slime. Of course, it synchronized with water. I was going to have them create a flow in the water by synchronizing with the water in the tank and staying active to keep the water flowing through the filter slime. They made the perfect, no-maintenance filtration system! I had even acquired water slimes that *use* water magic from the same slimes from Fatoma. But that was another story.

"Now to fill the tank..." One down, and I went on to work on the rest. Keeping them too uniform would not have been fun, so I switched up the scaping to make it interesting. Before I knew it, I had come to my last task. "Then I'll move this here…"

"Master Ryoma, it's almost time for lunch," Lilian called.

"Already?" Time seemed to fly, lately. That's the way it goes when I was doing things I enjoyed for work, I supposed. "This is the last one, so I'll wrap it up. I'll take my lunch in the dining hall."

"Yes, sir. The planters you have ordered have arrived."

"Can you keep them out of the way for now? I'll plant weed slimes in them for decoration. Can I leave you in charge of placing them around the building? I just need one per room."

Then, it'll be complete. A slime-based security system disguised as indoor plants and aquariums designed to keep track of the traffic inside the building. This meant I had also finished preparing the trap to snare our prey when it walked into the building.

■　　■　　■

That evening, I was standing in the courtyard shortly after sundown. A barrier kept the evening chill out, and there were enough lights set up along the wall. The grass below my feet was freshly cut and soft, enough to lessen the impact of anyone who might trip and fall out here.

"Sorry to keep you waiting, Boss."

In that courtyard, I was standing face to face with Hudom.

∼ **Chapter 7 Episode 29** ∼
The Match against Hudom

"I'm sorry to call you up on such short notice."

"I'm always down for a bit of sparring."

Hudom had traveled the lands in pursuit of mastering his martial artistry, and I had once promised him a sparring match. Even if Hudom had invented this backstory, it worked in my favor. I had called him to the courtyard, asking him to help with my training. Now, we faced each other in our street clothes, empty handed. Of course, my street clothes were a blade-proof shirt made from sticky slime silk, a hidden iron slime (weapon) in my belt, and safety boots in preparation for the worst.

"How's this for rules?" he asked. "No weapons, and no offensive or defensive magic. Enhancement spells and energy are allowed."

"Sounds good. Let's get started." I shook my limbs and stood in a comfortable stance as Hudom stood ten feet away, holding up both fists. It looked like a boxing stance, but his legs were spread a bit wider and his feet were firmly on the ground.

"Let's start!" As soon as he said so, he closed the distance between us in a leap, keeping the momentum in his punch.

But no magic or energy. I wondered for a moment whether he was going easy or just waiting to see what I would do.

"You'd throw a punch like that at a child...?"

"That's rich, since you dodged it like it was nothing!"

He was as fast and powerful as anything I'd seen on TV in my previous life. He threw punch after punch, becoming faster and in more complex combinations.

A fist came straight for my face, to which I stepped back barely out of reach. He immediately pulled back his right fist, and I followed it to get close. His other fist came at me, which I deflected with my right hand, turning myself ninety degrees in the process to try and strike him with my left fist. I timed the attack so he had no time to parry, but Hudom coolly put more distance between us to regroup.

From that point, we continued exchanging strikes. When he pushed, I pushed back, and when I pushed, he pushed back. Once in a while we mixed in kicks, but neither of us reached for big moves that would give the other an opening. Boring was one way to put it, but our exchanges were honest and straightforward. Just when we had gotten into a routine of taking turns attacking and responding...

Hudom's stance changed - his center of gravity lowered and his fists unfurled. Then, he leapt at me like a carnivore pouncing on its prey. I reflexively grabbed his hands, locking us into a grapple. He immediately used his height advantage to try and pin me to the ground; I relaxed for a second and took half a step back. Bending my elbows, I twisted his arms outwards as I ducked under him...

That was close. I had almost locked his joints, which would have limited his movement. Hudom had torn his hands free at the last second and put more distance between us.

"I wasn't holding back..." he said.

"I know a few grapples and throws myself."

"That's great to hear from my training partner."

The air about Hudom changed. I sensed his physical energy enveloping him as he took deep breaths. I showed my intent to retaliate by wearing my own energy.

Hudom smiled. "Here I come!"

His attacks became far more unpredictable; sometimes he transitioned from strikes to grapples or throws, and other times he mixed in strikes in a series of grapples and throws. He had so much variety in his attacks that it was fun to watch and parry. I also acknowledged that he must have trained for a long time to master those moves. At the very least, I was now sure that his experience and passion for martial arts was not just a backstory.

Out of respect, I decided to give this match my all. When he grabbed me, I pulled his arm to throw him off balance. When he low kicked me, I kicked back with the same leg to make him trip... I used the muscle memory from my previous life as much as I could. Hudom ended up deflected, thrown, and tossed to the ground over and over again. But, the light never faded from Hudom's eyes, nor did he ever stop moving.

Then, something strange happened. We had exchanged a series of strikes, creating a bit of distance between us. On his next punch, I sensed the energy around his fist strengthen, and I felt the fist that should never have reached me strike my shoulder. While the impact wasn't too strong, it was enough to stun me for an instant, combined with the surprise that the punch had reached me. Hudom, of course, did not miss that opportunity. He grappled me to the ground. I managed to kick and toss him behind me, still befuddled by the mysterious punch.

As we continued our match, I discovered that the attack was a kind of energy shot, where he could send and hit me with his energy. With renewed interest and excitement, I became lost in the match before I knew it…

■　■　■

The match ended with Hudom running out of stamina. Apparently, using energy for direct attacks used a lot more stamina than enhancing his strength. He was doing fine at first, but he started to lose speed with every energy shot towards the end.

Finally, Hudom fell to his knees, surrendered, and fell on his back, gazing up at the sky. He looked like he was happy with the match, having given it his all.

I handed Hudom a towel and a drink from my Item Box; he was almost wheezing. "There's a barrier to keep some of the cold out, but stay like that for too long and you'll catch your death."

Hudom waited a few seconds before answering, "Thanks…" He wiped his sweat with the towel and downed the contents of the cup. I assumed he was a little dazed from exhaustion. "That's good!"

"I'm glad to hear." I took out my own cup and the pitcher and served myself a glass of citrus-infused water. Its aroma was refreshing after that great exercise. I served Hudom and myself a second glass, allowing him to slowly hydrate and recuperate. "Better?" I asked.

"Much." Suddenly, he looked at me with a serious expression I hadn't seen on him before. "Thank you. I'm having trouble getting the words out... But that was a great experience." I felt sincere respect from him, as one martial artist shows another.

"Likewise. That was a great experience for me. I had never seen those energy moves before."

"Really? I'm glad you had something to gain from it."

"Would you like to have regular matches like this? I would like to learn more about those energy techniques."

"That would be awesome! There's plenty of things I want to learn from you too! Like..." He went on, more like himself but still just as passionate about martial arts.

We spent some time discussing what aspects we wanted to study. He said he had considered calling me "master" to learn from me, but that wasn't my style, so I proposed that we help each other grow. According to Hudom, that was a generous offer.

"Fighting techniques are the livelihood of many people. Most wouldn't give away that information to someone who isn't your apprentice."

Classes and training sessions were open to all at the Adventurers' Guild; those served the purpose of improving the survival and success rates of the local adventurers. Even then, most training only covered the basics unless some instructors or veteran adventurers decided to provide further instruction for personal reasons. There was pretty much no chance that anyone would give away proprietary techniques.

Even on Earth, I had heard that many martial arts dojos were very secretive about their techniques, even going as far as banning their students from training with anyone outside of the dojo and having them sign an oath upon their joining. There were plenty of other measures they took, from designing a set of "show" techniques for anyone outside of the dojo, teaching techniques that require oral instruction from the master to fully understand, etc. Considering how much importance martial arts of yesteryear placed on secrecy, it felt a bit unfair that anyone in the modern day could look up most martial arts forms or techniques in books or online.

I understood Hudom's point, but felt I must share the open-information philosophy of modern-day Earth.

"Just keep it in the back of your mind," he said. "It's a great deal for me, and there are some martial arts that are very open about their techniques."

"Right... Wait, that reminds me."

"Something wrong?"

I had completely forgotten the real reason I was here. "I didn't ask you to come here just to train, you know."

"Oh?"

"There's something I want to ask you."

"I'll answer anything I can."

"Wonderful. You're selling information on me, aren't you? Who are you selling it to?"

Hudom was happening to be finishing his glass of citrus water, and the question caused the drink to go down his windpipe.

"How do you—"

"You may know that the recent rise in crime in the city has been manufactured. Nobles who oppose the duke are surely behind it. So, we'd been laying a trap to catch their agents red handed."

"And I stepped in the trap."

"More importantly, the person you were giving the information to."

Hudom instantly looked deflated, then, perhaps from guilt, determination lit up his face.

"Um... I don't think I'm about to do what you're expecting me to."

"What?"

"Truth be told, there were suggestions to capture you without having this conversation, but I insisted on giving us this opportunity. I had this feeling... And the training session was just an excuse, but I got carried away... I'm sorry about that."

I looked up at the roof and saw a small, owl-like monster there; I had been told it was Lilian's familiar. I had only found out the previous day that Lilian was a tamer.

"It's true that I've been giving away information on you, so why talk to me?"

"Oh, yes. We know you have, and I trust the report I received. I just don't know who you are giving the information to, so I don't necessarily see you as an enemy yet."

"Still, most people *would* see you that way for blabbing about you behind your back."

"I suppose so." That's why it took me a long time to convince the room yesterday. On top of Lilian's familiar keeping watch, I had set up the slime security this morning, and made sure to wear my full-armor street clothes. There were other tricks set up in the courtyard as well, and I could duck out at any time with space magic. In that case, Hughes and the security instructor would come rushing in.

"I had to propose all of these safety measures just to be allowed to do this. And everyone only reluctantly agreed."

"That's the normal reaction. Why did you go through the trouble?"

I didn't exactly know why. "I might not have known you for long, so I can only say that I felt like you weren't an enemy. Just an intuition. I was actually just given advice from someone that I was too logical in my decision-making and I had to trust my instinct." While it was true that it didn't feel like Hudom was an enemy, I couldn't help but think of things logically. When I did, I felt like

I was trying to use logic to convince myself he wasn't a threat. "Anyway! I don't know exactly why, but I followed my intuition. That's why I set this conversation up."

"You're pretty wild…"

"I've had all of that and meaningful looks from people already, so there's no use telling me that now." I was trained for this in my previous life! You need thick skin and brazenness to survive an abusive work environment. "So, I would like to hear your side of the story, but please make it quick. I'm keeping them waiting, worried about me. They could come storming in any minute without waiting for my signal. Tell me now! Please!"

"All right, all right! I don't need this pressure on me!" Once I stopped rushing him, Hudom sighed.

"So, what do you want to know…" he muttered.

"Who's paying you, or rather, who's seeking information on me. Just tell me what you know."

"That's easy."

He proceeded to give me the name and title of the individual in question; for a moment, I thought my ears were failing me.

"Did I just hear that right? *Who* were you giving my information to?"

"His Majesty, Erias De Rifall."

⇌ Chapter 7 Episode 30 ⇌
Hudom's Reasons

~Hudom's Side~

Once I informed him that I was giving information about him to His Majesty, he asked me again, "Does that mean you're a spy...?"

"We *do* have those departments, of course, but I'm just His Majesty's personal errand boy."

It looked like I'd better start at the beginning. I expressed this sentiment, and he permitted me to take my time. I wasn't going to drag it out, but this was going to take a while regardless. It all started in my school days, after all. Just before my graduation.

"At the time, I was fighting with my dad almost every day. He was adamantly against me pursuing martial arts or traveling to test myself... I told you a bit about my family before."

"They were a generation of royal gardeners."

"That's all you need to know. One day during that time in my life pops called me out to his *office*." I was younger back then, and I was just mad at him... I thought he was going to boast about the job and scold me for entertaining the ridiculous aspiration of mine... "I didn't want to go, but blowing him off would have felt like running away. So I showed up as I was told, and His Majesty was waiting for me. I discovered there that His Majesty and my pops had secretly been close since he was a gardener in training. When pops told His Majesty about me, he saw an opportunity."

"Opportunity?"

"His Majesty received piles of reports containing various pieces of information from all over the country. Those, however, had been sorted and refined by several subordinates and deemed worthy of His Majesty's time and attention. That was partially because His Majesty could never get through all of the reports on his own, but he wanted more unrefined information. Straight from the horse's mouth. The uncensored voice of the people."

His Majesty had been notoriously free spirited since youth. He had made friends with my dad because he was hiding in the garden to get away from his studies.

"That certainly speaks to the king's character," my boss said. "And the relationship between you and your father... No wonder you're his errand boy."

"Right. Naturally, once His Majesty inherited the throne, it was much harder for him to sneak out of the palace. So, I would travel the lands and regularly report to him the status of the cities and areas I passed through. In exchange for me taking on this task, His Majesty helped convince my father to allow my departure." And just so he knew... "The information I give is only things a normal traveler would see. Mostly the atmosphere of the city and any rumors going around. The espionage you're thinking of is reserved for professionals trained in that department, and that doesn't include me."

Something seemed to click with the boss. Before I could ask what that was, he threw another question at me.

"Why did you choose my laundry shop for your cover? I remember hearing that you helped Chelma the cook, and that led to the job... And that you needed to make some money before resuming your travels."

"That was a coincidence. I had come to Gimul under His Majesty's direction, but I happened to help a lady in need and decided to walk her back since the city didn't look too safe. Not to mention, I needed the money. The only payment I received from His Majesty was him persuading my father."

"Really?"

"He offered, but my father and I refused. My father did kind of goad me into it when we were ironing out our deal... My journey was supposed to be my chance to improve myself. There was no point in embarking on it if someone else had to foot the bill." That reminded me. "In exchange, I guess, I have been given the freedom to choose where I go, for the most part. This is the first time I've been asked to go to a specific city. And, the information I gather is usually sent in a letter to my father, which is then passed on to the throne. This time, though, a contact is stationed in the city. I received a response to my letter one time, so I assume the contact or someone else uses space magic to deliver my letters to His Majesty straight away."

"The throne is more involved this time... Can you tell me why?"

"Apparently, the rumor that crime is rising here has been quietly spreading among nobles. His Majesty caught wind of it..." All of a sudden, the boss's expression darkened, now looking quiet but ominous.

"The rumor's widespread. I rushed back to Gimul after hearing the same rumor in Fatoma."

Come to think of it, he seemed even more on edge now than he was when we first met... Not that I needed to quell his anger, but I decided to add, "It's not uncommon for news of scandals to spread quickly. Especially if the rumors are backed up by fact."

"And if not, facts can be manufactured."

"Exactly." He was quick to catch on... I was a bit worried that the glimmer in his eyes seemed to fade out. "Boss?"

"Oh, sorry. I was just thinking of something... Next question. You're telling me that your job was to report on the city, but I've heard that you were looking into me. Can you explain this?"

"It's true that I was looking into you specifically, but I *can* explain that."

"Go ahead."

I finally got to say what I had been thinking these past few days. "It's because you're doing too bloody much!"

I mean, I wasn't lying that my assignment was gathering intel and rumors about the *city*, but still!

"I go out into the city to gather information, and all everyone can talk about is you! What choice do I have but to look into you?!"

When I asked people what was troubling them, most mentioned the laborers or rise in crime, which inevitably led to the security company and trash plant that he started, or about the rezoning of the slums. When they talked about him, they told me everything: how close he was with the duke, how he used incredible magic and kept a countless variety of slimes, and even where I could usually find him at any given time or day; things I hadn't even asked about. "It was no more an investigation than it was confirming public knowledge! No matter how far I dug, I got no further than what the lady at the grocery shop told me at the start! Why don't you post everything about yourself in the town square while you're at it?!"

"Right. I thought it might have gone like that... Can't argue with you there." At least he was self-aware of how much attention he was drawing. He also seemed satisfied with my defense. "Thank you for letting me know. I think that's about all I wanted to ask... Well, one more question. Not that you can do anything about it now, but are you okay with telling me everything like this? You didn't even hesitate."

"I thought being honest was the best option for me."

Every noble knew that the king and the Jamils (especially the current duke) were close. My boss could easily verify everything I just told him, including my history and my family. My job wasn't something I should brag about, but it also wasn't important enough to try and conceal. "As soon as you lured me in here, I had nowhere to run. Any half-baked lie would only hurt me in the end."

"I understand. Thank you," he said, and slowly waved his hands.

Immediately, an armed group came flooding in from the doors on all four sides. I thought they were coming to restrain me, but—

"Please lower your guard, Master Hudom. If you remain calm, so will we." A calm voice rang in the courtyard. It came from Lulunese, the maid who showed me to the courtyard; I just recalled her name when I saw her face behind the armed men and women. True to her word, the group had only surrounded me but made no further move to arrest or hurt me. "I ensured that we could hear the conversation between you and Master Ryoma."

"That's true," the boss politely said to me before turning to the crowd. "What do you all think of Hudom's explanation?"

The men close to him answered first. If memory served, they were the ones sent by the duke; I had seen them around the laundry shop a few times.

"I don't think we need to take him by force, at least. You guys got way too into your match, anyway. Looking like you were having a blast. Took the wind out of our sails."

"S-Sorry about that."

"It's fine, as long as you're safe. When it comes to his story... Jill?"

"Invoking His Majesty's name is a serious matter. Depending on the situation, the mere mention of his name without his permission could constitute a crime... Which would be highly likely in this case. This would lead to damaging his family name if word got out, and many houses would cut off or severely punish anyone who committed such a crime. His punishment would be far less severe to pretend he did it for the money." She opened her mouth to add something, but said, "No, we should make sure of it first. Now, Hudom. You are going to come with us. We were watching you during your *conversation* with Ryoma, which he had insisted on organizing. As a result, we see you as much less of a threat than before. That being said, we can't let you walk free just yet. We'll need to ask you some questions of our own. You understand."

"Of course." She made it sound like she wouldn't take no for an answer towards the end, but I deserved that implication in this situation. I showed that I was ready to follow without a fight, and he ordered the group to move indoors.

"All right... Thank you. I had fun, and I appreciate your consideration."

"I only wanted to satisfy my curiosity. I'll see you tomorrow."

After he left, I simply followed the way they showed me as I wondered what awaited me.

"What's with the weird look? Do you regret it?" Hughes asked.

Did I really have a weird look on my face?

"I don't regret it."

I had agreed to work for His Majesty of my own volition. Even if it was just relaying little rumors, I did feel joy and pride that I was directly serving the king. Moreover, the work allowed me to live my life as I wanted to. I didn't regret my decision, but... "I had a lot

104

of fun tonight. I only have myself to blame, but I'm sorry things had to end this way."

"You said you were honest about why you started traveling, and you both looked genuinely happy."

"It wasn't much fun for us watching from the shadows."

"Cut him some slack, Jill."

"No. The match never would have happened if I had my way. Ryoma's safety is our top priority, and we let them duke it out one on one... What if he had been the type of person to take Ryoma hostage?!"

Ha! I had to agree, it wasn't the safest option. But... "I couldn't have done it if I tried."

"True, Ryoma has incredible strength, especially for his age. But nothing was guaranteed." He seemed a bit overprotective, despite his stoic attitude.

"He was stronger than I had expected." I had given it my all in the way of martial arts and improved my skills over my journey. While I knew I was still young, I had experienced plenty of fights, wins and losses, and I felt that I'd earned some confidence through my experience. I gave it my all, and he crushed me. Like I was a child challenging an adult.

I felt a sort of history through his technique, but more so the skills required to wield those moves in combat, and even more so the training he must have undergone to build those skills. I felt that weight behind every move. I had always thought that he didn't act like a typical child his age, but towards the end, I saw no child at all. All I saw was a man who had honed his skills for decades. He just happened to take on the form of a child. Maybe that doesn't make sense. Maybe my brain was still recovering from the exhaustion of our match. But, somehow, I had gotten that impression. This helped me accept my defeat, and admitting it out loud came easy. To meet someone like him was why I set out on my journey in the first place, and my greatest pleasure to do so.

I didn't know what punishment I would face. Fired from the laundry shop, for starters, I assumed. I might not be allowed near him again. Getting involved with any noble issue, not just the Jamils, always spelled trouble... I doubted they would go as far as to kill me, but it was possible that I would be detained for a while. What was I going to do...?

■ ■ ■

The next day, after spending the night in a room within the security company's headquarters, I was shown to a different room after breakfast.

"Good morning. Oh? Did you get some rest last night?"

My boss was there, acting like nothing had happened.

He even added, "Hudom, I'm reassigning you. Going forward, I would like you to guard me, instead of the laundry shop. Sorry I couldn't give you more advance notice."

How did it come to this...?

❧ Chapter 7 Episode 31 ❧
Guard Duty and Small Talk

"What's going on?" Hudom clearly didn't understand the situation. He was looking dumbfoundedly back and forth between me and Jill, who had brought him here.

I decided to give him a quick explanation. "After our match last night and the questioning that followed, we determined that you most likely are not our enemy, nor do you intend me any harm."

"Not *for now*, at least. We are still vetting your story through the duke, who is currently in the capital. If possible, he will ask His Majesty about you directly," Jill added.

"That's where we're at. It will take some time before we have our final verdict. But don't you think it would be a detriment to both of us to keep you detained or locked up somewhere that entire time?"

Hudom would lose his freedom while I would have to allocate some of my workforce on top of losing Hudom as a member of the team.

"I agree, but I had looked into your private information and gave it away without your permission…"

"Yes, you did. That's why I decided to have you work under my watch rather than back at the laundry shop or any of the new businesses. As I've explained, we deemed you as safe to have around me."

Hudom turned to Jill with a doubtful expression.

"We *are* short-staffed," Jill said, "but the number one reason is Ryoma's request."

"I can't afford to ignore someone who has a good background and who I can trust to a certain degree, especially under these circumstances. I even proposed for whoever is stationed as your contact here to work with us, but everyone was strongly against that."

"For the record, that's the *sane* reaction!"

"I haven't done anything wrong, so I don't mind. I'm going to the trouble of keeping things legal and peaceful." If I wasn't, I could have beaten up Wanz and anyone else we were sure was involved back at the conference.

"You have a sinister look on your face, boss."

"Oh, sorry. My decision is final, so..."

"We tried talking him out of it, but he was too stubborn... Just consider yourself lucky."

The two adults with us wore a bitter expression and a confused one respectively, concluding this process. Let's get to work.

"Now that you've brought me out here, what are we going to do?" Hudom asked.

"I have a meeting with the guildmasters at the Merchants' Guild in the afternoon. We're going to take a stroll around the city until then. It'll be a decent walk. Are you feeling okay?"

"My head's still spinning, but I'm fine physically. I'll do your guard duty to the best of my ability. That seems like a better deal for me than worrying about it."

Looks like Hudom was ready for a fresh start. He might have been my guard, but I didn't want to be all formal, so we continued with the small talk as we made our way there.

"I'm counting on you. Jill tells me that you were a great student enrolled in the knight's path."

"Oh, you heard? I don't have many pleasant memories about it... I was always rebelling against inheriting the family position, even before I set my heart on martial arts. My father always told me to make decent grades so I could support myself..."

"Even so, I hear it's a program that takes a lot of dedication."

According to Jill, the academy in the capital had various "paths," or departments, where students could take classes aligning with their interests or career paths. Anyone could register for these classes as long as they paid the tuition and had passed the prerequisite course or test. The knight's path, however, was a bit exceptional in that qualifying for the program was a feat in and of itself.

"I'm told that the student needs to be of noble birth, and excel in the academics like etiquette, general knowledge, history, and magic theory, as well as combat skills in magic, hand-to-hand, and weapons...and have a *respectable* appearance."

"Well... The course is designed to train knights that would protect the country and the royal family. It is very demanding. Only the top thirty of eligible students are enrolled each year, and being enrolled doesn't guarantee anything. If you can't keep up with the courses, you'll be kicked out. If some of the eligible students scored similarly, they would compete against each other to stay in the program, all the way until graduation."

In exchange for the tough requirements and strict meritocracy, those who graduated were on the shortest path to becoming a royal knight, serving in the Knights' Order, or taking on an important post in the army. The knight's path was the most prestigious and difficult path in the academy. I assumed *decent* grades wouldn't cut it to get into a program like that, but Hudom still seemed sour about his time in it.

"I did put in a lot of work, but..."

"Something you don't want to talk about?"

"Nothing good ever came from me saying this... Most people just groan, and I thought I was going to be killed when I told my classmates on the knight's path."

Uh-oh. I wasn't going to push it if he didn't want to say, but now I was really curious.

"I can tell you," Hudom reassured. "Part of working hard in the knight's path had to do with my parents bugging me about my grades and out of concern for my future, but the biggest reason for me... Well, girls go crazy for guys in the knight's path." He awkwardly chuckled.

"That makes sense," I said.

"I hope I didn't offend you, but do I come across that sleazy?"

"You do seem experienced. I heard you were popular with female customers at the laundry shop, so that was a positive for me."

"Really?"

"Yes. And isn't finding a spouse important to nobles? I may be generalizing...but I think many women are very realistic when it comes to that. I think they look for men with a respectable family, finances, and income potential. Men who don't meet those criteria may not even be considered suitable candidates for marriage."

"I guess it depends, but I know some people are very cut and dried about that kind of stuff."

Then maybe it wasn't a mistake for Hudom to join the knight's path. It seemed like he decided to pursue martial arts shortly before his graduation. Before that, there were plenty of paths for his future: becoming a knight, taking a different kind of job, or even marrying.

"You joined the knight's path that offered you a lot of possibilities for the future. You said you wanted female attention, but you put in the work that allowed you to join, and considering possibilities of marriage, it wasn't the wrong move. I think it was a great decision." At this point, I realized Hudom was looking at me wide-eyed. "Is something wrong?"

"No one's ever put it like that. I'm a bit surprised."

I hadn't expected that.

"I haven't told this to many people to begin with," Hudom went on. "My classmates, teachers, and my family... Most of them scolded me, saying that I couldn't possibly become a knight with that kind of mindset. When there was a teacher or upperclassman in the path, they made me run laps around the academy."

"Does the knight's path emphasize mentality in training? Like, they won't let you drink water during training?"

"Yeah, that was the feeling you'd get. The teacher was always shouting at us to 'tough it out!'"

I was starting to equate the knight's path to a high school sports team of yesteryear Japan. Hudom noticed where our destination was.

"Aren't we headed to the open area of the slums?"

"Yes. If all went well, there should be new buildings finished this morning."

"Another new project?"

"A few food service establishments."

"Food service? Don't all of your businesses include food in your employee's pay?"

"They do. But once my employees have the necessities, I figured they might want to splurge once in a while."

Maybe a special occasion, a reward to themselves, a celebration, or even just to mix up their diet once in a while.

"I decided to put up a few restaurants near the dorms. The themes are 'comfort food' and 'cheap and filling.'"

"I understand why you'd want the former. What about the latter?"

"The latter is aimed for workers who don't have as much money yet. We have hired a lot of them, but there are plenty more workers on the streets and more coming into the city."

"I see. It's for newcomers and people that you can't guarantee the necessities to."

"Right. We're building more lodgings for the same target."

I was thinking of beef bowl stands, Japanese diners, and packed lunch shops. Back in Japan, especially when I was young, being able to fill my stomach for cheap was a comfort in itself. For the lodgings, I pictured capsule hotels from a generation ago, which would serve as the bare-minimum shelter for as many people as possible.

"So more workers are coming in," Hudom said. "Even though you've managed to bring down the crime rate significantly."

"Several of the nobles are in cahoots, and the fact that laborers are coming in from all over means that there are many people involved in the process... My guess is that they don't want to back down."

"They may be cooperating, but only in a limited capacity. Maybe it'll take time for them to coordinate their next move."

"The duke's people have listed five names with possible involvement: Baron Ransor, Baron Reefled, Viscount Fargatton, Viscount Danielton, and Count Sandrick. Personally, I also suspect Baron Gerock, Viscount Anatoma, Viscount Geromon, Viscount Sergil, and Count Bernard."

"Where'd you get that idea...? Sounds like you didn't get those names from the duke or his people," Hudom asked, carefully looking around.

It was simple. I was hiring a lot of the workers coming into Gimul. As an employer, I have access to their résumé, and of course, I do go over them. At the very least, their résumé told me where they were from. When some of the locations kept popping up, I started remembering them.

"People leaving their territory isn't a good sign for a lord, is it?"

"It's a detriment to the tax income and workforce. It's not uncommon for lords to forbid their population to move residences unless permitted, especially when it comes to leaving their land. Most of them would be moving for temporary gigs, but there are so many that you have hired alone. Can't deny the possibility of the lords encouraging this, somehow. Even if it's as passive as *not* forbidding their migration."

"Right. So it's only a suspicion now. But it's not my job to follow through on that."

"You want me to notify His Majesty?"

"Oh, no. I won't stick my nose in your business. A royal order is way beyond my pay grade… Besides everything I've noticed, I've told someone who works for the duke, so he is aware and is making his move. With that in mind, it's up to you if you want to tell the king."

"Up to me? If I don't report it now, it'll look like I hid it… You're absolutely going to take advantage of my post," Hudom said with resignation, but followed his statement with a smile.

⮜ Chapter 7 Episode 32 ⮞
Advice from Taylor

In the afternoon, a meeting was held as scheduled in a boardroom within the Merchants' Guild with the seven representatives of each relevant department: the three guildmasters, Dameyer the chief of security in the city, Arnold who was at the top of the bureaucracy, the leader of the slums Lible, and me.

Two hours were spent on the meeting, leaving me with thirty extra minutes that I had blocked out for it. I took the opportunity to ask branch manager Taylor about Sensory Sharing.

"That must be the monster's vision. A slime's vision, in your case. I'll call it vision, even though it's technically magical detection, but 'vision' in the sense that it is what the monster sees. First of all, you don't see exactly what a monster sees through Sensory Sharing. It may sound obvious, but us humans and our monsters don't share the same anatomy."

I hadn't thought about that. The anatomy of our sensory receptors were different. Humanoid monsters like goblins were one thing, but I doubted that a limour bird and I were truly seeing the same things, so to speak.

"Humans and monsters may be looking at the same view, but won't share the same vision. Unless…"

"Unless the taming magic converts the vision into something humans can process?"

"Exactly. The effect of our contract is to enable communication with monsters. In addition to communicating commands from tamer to monster, it also communicates the monster's feelings to the tamer. In the same way, Sensory Sharing converts visual data from the monster to a form the tamer can understand. But you, Ryoma, during your experimentation, must have glimpsed into the *true* vision of a slime... A world sensed only by magic detection."

That sounded like my theory that slimes observe their surroundings with magic was correct!

"I hate to take the wind out of your sails, but if you intend to keep studying this, you should be aware of something," Taylor jumped in. "I haven't heard any tales of anyone else trying to pull off what you are, so I can't be certain about this, but if a human were to attempt to process all of their sensory information through one single magical sense instead of the usual five senses, it could very well cause a sensory overload. You did fall ill rather quickly from all the information the slime was feeding to you, right?"

That made sense, and I appreciated his concern. I promised that I would be careful during my experiments.

"Good," he said. "On another matter, I heard you started keeping goblins. You registered eight, I believe."

"Yes. I detained goblins robbing my farm, so I contracted them to help with my work and the slimes."

"How is it going? Are you getting along with them well?"

"Well... I can communicate with them, although not as smoothly as I do with the slimes. And I established a clear dynamic when I first detained them, so they've never tried to rebel. You could say we're getting along well, but..." There was something on my mind.

"But?"

"They seem different from the goblins I've seen before. They're very calm, and we never have any tension. The quieter they are the better, so I haven't been too concerned."

"Hm... How do you mean 'calm,' exactly? And how do you usually interact with them?"

"What I want from them is labor, so I have them do all kinds of work. Nothing too dangerous. I've forbidden them from leaving the mountain or attacking anyone, but they are free, otherwise. They are also very honest with what they want. If they find the work engaging or pleasant, they learn it more quickly. I tried to show them how each task can benefit them."

When I first taught them how to tend the farm, for example, I used my magic to rapidly grow the crops so I could show them that their work would lead to a full meal. They had been nearly naked, but once I showed them that wearing clothes could keep them warm, they began wearing clothes without me having to tell them to. They used to eat the crops raw when they were hungry until I served them a hot meal. After that, they started asking and waiting for hot meals. I even showed them that using utensils would keep their hands from getting hot when eating their food, and they had started using them.

"I started ordering them to bathe to keep them clean, and those who liked it started taking baths twice a day without me telling them to. Once they tasted a prototype batch of the alcohol I started making recently, some of them started prepping more alcohol like they were trying to fill an entire mine, all in their free time... Just two days ago, they came up with the luxurious idea of drinking in the bath, which made them get wasted there. I told them that alcohol hits harder when you're bathing and gave them a stern warning not to do it again. That's the only problem I've encountered, I suppose."

As it crossed my mind that I might have to establish a drinking limit with the goblins, I noticed that Taylor was looking at me with a kind but pitiful gaze. "I'm sorry, I got carried away."

"That's all right. It doesn't sound like you are having any issues that I was concerned about. You can't hope for better than to form a good relationship with peaceful goblins, albeit on the indulgent side."

Indulgent! That's what those goblins reminded me of. The videos of animals at zoos in Japan being described as having lost their feral nature. Domesticated goblins...didn't have the same charm as those animals, but the same principles applied.

"The low population of the goblins is also a factor," Taylor said, producing a set of writing utensils to write or draw out his points.

Goblins were not too dangerous on their own. They were weak monsters to begin with, but they also prioritized avoiding danger, and satisfying their hunger when alone. With survival at the top of their minds, they rarely attacked other creatures. As their numbers in a group increased past a dozen or so, they grew more and more violent, beginning to hunt to provide enough food for the pack. They hunted small animals while their group was smaller, but larger groups hunted medium-sized prey, which included humans. When they became a horde of a hundred-plus, more violent, weapon-wielding species like the archer goblin, and strong, human-sized ones like the hobgoblin, were born.

From that point, the weapon-wielding species would lead large groups to defend their horde or hunt for food while the hobgoblins contributed to manual labor to rapidly expand their horde. After some time, advanced species like goblin knights that are both powerful and weapon-wielding emerge. In the end, they'd become a massive army with a "king" at their helm. I had been told that advanced species were more likely to be born in larger hordes, but not that they would become more violent as their numbers grew.

"They become more brazen in groups. They're a bit like humans," I remarked.

"If their ruler is dangerous, the entire group is dangerous. Not much different from humans. That's why it's important for the tamer to have a firm grip on their reins. And I'm glad you do, Ryoma. Don't let your guard down with them. Also, the sprint-rabbit license exam is coming up in a week. Are you ready?"

"I think so. Everyone's been kind enough to help me make time to study. One of the duke's maids has the license, so she's been tutoring me."

"Glad to hear. As a proctor, I can't disclose too much about the exam... But sprint rabbits are not too powerful, nor dangerous. So why is a license required to keep or breed them?"

"Because they breed rapidly and have a great appetite, they are likely to cause great damage to farms and their crops if they become feral, which can happen without proper care."

"Correct. That's the most important principle. Make sure to review specific guidelines for care and specifications for housing. If possible, you should research records of past and current sprint rabbit farms."

Well, I couldn't pass up on a tip from the top man of the Tamers' Guild! I would use it to revise before the exam.

Shortly after, we reached the end of our scheduled meeting, formally adjourning it.

～ Chapter 7 Episode 33 ～
Small Talk on the Way Home,
and the Current State of the City

I met up with my bodyguard Hudom at the reception area of the guild.

"I'm sorry for the wait."

"Oh. Meeting's over?"

"Yes. It went smoothly."

I had him wait for me in the reception area during the meeting.

"Th-Then, I should be getting back to work," said one of the receptionists. Apparently, Hudom and she had been speaking.

"Did I interrupt?"

"Just chatting. And gathering intel. What's next on the agenda?"

"Cleaning the streets in the afternoon, but there's still some time. I was going to stop by the security headquarters. I've left capable hands at each post, but I need to review and sign some paperwork."

"Roger that."

Just as Hudom reached for the front door of the Merchants' Guild, I made eye contact with a man walking into the building. Disgust flashed on his face for a split second before it immediately snapped into a smile as he called, "My, my. Long time no see."

"Hello, Wanz."

"We haven't spoken since the unfortunate conclusion to our conference. You seem well."

"Yes, thank you. Have you lost some weight, by any chance?"

"With the cold weather coming in quickly... Fancy seeing you here."

"I came by to see a friend."

"I see. It's the same for me. Excuse me."

"Take care."

Wanz headed to the reception desk as we headed outside. He apparently wanted to avoid conversations with me as much as I did with him. Just an ostentatious greeting out of obligation.

"Boss, you called him Wanz?"

"He's the one."

"He is the one you ferociously debated back when you were all on edge. Glad that it went peacefully."

"I wasn't going to start arguing with him then and there. Looks like he wants to keep playing the innocent, law-abiding citizen."

"Oh?" Hudom peered into my face. "And why are you feeling down? I'm sure you didn't want to meet that guy, but did he get you that upset?"

"Do I look that upset?"

"Yes."

It must have been written all over my face. "Well, I hadn't seen him since the debate, and I don't understand why I went as far as I did against someone like that. I can't really explain it... But when I first met him, I felt this pressure...like I had to stop him at all costs."

"Pressure from him?"

"I'm not sure. I just felt like I couldn't let things go like he wanted them to."

But I didn't feel that way at all when I bumped into him. I couldn't understand why I was so stressed out about it in the conference. It even felt excessive to me for me to have reacted so drastically. It *was* excessive, I suppose.

"It's like I was facing a single goblin with plenty of allies on my side, and I should have gone at it with enough caution to prevent injury, but I went in ready to die trying, somehow imagining that the entire nation would come crashing down if I would lose... I overreacted so badly to such a small threat that I want to go crawl in a hole! The more I think about it the more embarrassed I am, and I could say that I felt cornered or—"

"Got it. I understand that it's embarrassing for you to think about it."

I felt like this incident would be my worst memory of this life.

"Out of personal and professional curiosity... Should you do something about him?" Hudom asked after giving our surroundings a once-over.

I looked around myself before answering, "Our enemy is planting all sorts of traps to increase crime in Gimul. We're not going to beat them by eliminating lowly agents like Wanz."

Let's say we *could* get rid of Wanz, either legally by obtaining solid evidence of their wrongdoing, or by force without anyone knowing. What then? Unless we went after the nobles who controlled agents like Wanz, and the leader among them, there would only be more agents sent into the city until they gave up on the whole scheme. At this time, there is close to nothing that we could do against the nobles lurking behind the agents. Make a hasty attack against a noble, and we could easily be painted the villains. That being said...

"I have been told that the duke and duchess are already working on that front in the capital. There's no need for us to take a risk by jumping into action. They will unmask the puppeteer." Leave it to the experts, I'd say. "What we can do in this city now is to mitigate the crime in Gimul and the damage caused by it as much as possible until the duke and duchess accomplish their mission, hopefully bringing crime down to where it was before the large influx of workers. Otherwise, we will prepare for the worst-case scenario. In other words, we don't need to rush to cure the disease, only treat the symptoms."

Even during today's meeting, Dameyer had mentioned that the crime rate had dropped almost to where it was before the workers had come in. "There are still minor fights and conflicts attributed to the increase in population, but those are prevented from escalating because the patrol teams of the security company are using their large numbers to an advantage by making frequent rounds."

"Some of your staff are the laborers coming in, right? No wonder you have a lot of members."

"We're still regularly hiring."

Speaking of them, we just happened to pass a patrol unit as we were talking. A few paces later, I heard someone call to the team and thank them. My patrol officers had nearly become homeless themselves, but their honest work had garnered them a decent reception from the people of Gimul.

"I feel like the city has regained its old tranquility. We would need to keep our guard up, but I think we've avoided the worst-case scenario. Now, we just need to focus on preserving this state and trust that the duke and duchess will get to the source. The city is more important than dealing with that little puppet." Although, I had only reached this conclusion after hearing what Hughes and the other staff members had to say. "I've been told that the showdown will be during the year-end ball season, and victory is ours if we can make it that far. I took it as a show of confidence that they are going to nail the puppeteer within the year."

"Oh, it's because things have progressed that far."

"What is?"

"How calm you are compared to before. And no offense, but you don't seem as busy. Just a quick impression from my first day as your bodyguard, but…"

"It's not as bad as you thought?"

Hudom gave a timid nod, but I took no offense to it.

"I'm much calmer thanks to everyone coming over from the duke's, and I'm really not busy anymore. But I don't think that affects what's going on with the city."

"You're a central figure in the city now, Boss."

"Well… I gave my opinion here and there, but that's it. I did build the security company and the trash plant, and the slime product factory with the Morgan company, but I just gave my opinion and my money, and signed a few papers. I completely delegate the actual work to whoever's in charge." I really was doing this. All I had to do as owner was sign a summary of the business progressions, which didn't take much time at all. "I could say morning strolls like this are part of the job if I say I'm double checking that the notes I receive are accurate… Anyway, I definitely have enough breathing room that I wouldn't say I'm busy. I actually never feel like I'm working lately. For the most part, I use my time for my hobbies like researching slimes, or farm work, or studying for the license exam at the Tamers' Guild."

"You were just in a meeting."

Even those meetings were just an opportunity for me to listen to what they had to say and give my opinion on them. The ones putting in the real work would be the guildmasters and their people. Even before I built the security company, there were constables defending the city, and many people were working to enact policies that would help it. Even when crime was on the rise, the city's *self-cleansing* system was there in the form of people trying to improve their own situation. This time, however, the influx of workers had shut down those mechanisms, like a server overloaded with a flood of cyber attacks. I just had to lessen the load on each department. If the city was running out of jobs and lodgings to take these workers in, I just had to build more receptacles. Once the environment recovered enough for its self-cleansing mechanics to function, the crime rate would naturally improve.

"I suggest things like that, and push it through with money, power, and connections. When it's all said and done, I toss the project to capable hands. I'm definitely not as busy as everyone seems to think I am."

Since I had done a lot of flashy work on my own, people who knew what was going on might see me as a central figure of the city, but I doubted there was going to be much yield for him in trying to gain information from my life. In fact, wouldn't he lose time and effort, the more he put his focus on me? I voiced this concern, and Hudom returned a long sigh.

"Do people ever tell you how surprisingly evil you are?"

"Excuse you. Not that it's anything to be proud of, but I am easily manipulated and taken advantage of." That was only because I was surrounded by manipulators over my thirty-nine years on Earth, so I had learned their techniques by experience... No, that surely had nothing to do with this. "I'm not *evil*, come on. Let's return to the topic we were discussing before the meeting."

"Pretty obvious deflection, but all right. Weren't we talking about the moves I used in our match?"

"If you don't mind talking about it."

"None of them are secret techniques, and I was taught them by my trainer at the academy, so I don't mind sharing them."

"Thank you. If you're willing to teach me your techniques as well, I'll set a time and place for it. There's a lot I want to ask about, but I want to start with the one where you shot your energy at me."

"If you figured that out, there's not much I can tell you about… But you did use energy to strengthen your whole body."

"Yes. That's how I was taught to use energy."

"The first step is being able to fight normally while strengthening your whole body. It's the foundation, and you do that well. If you're able to beat your opponents with that, great. But you never know what will happen in battle. You could face an opponent much stronger, or harder to deal with. The necessity to prepare for the worst invented the moves I was using the other day. That's what I was told, anyway. The one where I shoot my energy at you, for example, is used to attack enemies outside the range of our fists or weapons. With enough skill, you can use that to fight against flying monsters or distant archers. Of course, nothing beats proper preparation. There are others, like one that strengthens your fist or weapon to hit monsters covered in hard shells. But the best master can only fully utilize his strength when his weapon is brought to its full potential. All of these techniques start with strengthening your body, and mastering them brings you back to strengthening your body. It's the foundation and ultimate goal of this series of techniques."

I was just about to mention how interesting that was when he continued, "And I made myself sound like an expert, but I'm far from it, so that was all hearsay. But, according to the legend of Tigar the Warrior God, his skin became an impenetrable armor with the use of energy, and his fists broke dragon scales. I say legend, but there are several documents to back this up."

"Oh…" It was a surprise to hear (as far as everyone knew) my grandfather's name out of nowhere. Hudom continued to tell me interesting stories about famous military men and adventurers of history. He was even more of an entertaining conversation partner than I had expected, making the walk back to the security company feel very short.

When we arrived, I was about to regretfully hit the pause button on our conversation to return to work when Lilian the maid called to us.

"Master Ryoma." She was standing at the reception desk, just out of the way. "Orest Moulton of the Moulton Slave Trading Company is here to see you."

"Orest?" The suspicious and good-looking president of the company? I was sure we didn't have an appointment.

"I told him of your absence, and he said it wasn't a problem, and that he had come without an appointment. He asked to wait for your return… He is in the meeting room now. Should I dismiss him?"

"No, I'll see him if he's waiting for me."

I wanted to know what he wanted, and I owed him one from last time… Still, I had a feeling that our meeting wasn't going to go too easily. With my guard up, I headed up to the meeting room.

⇐ Chapter 7 Episode 34 ⇒
Lunch with Orest

After the meeting with the guildmasters, I had returned to the security company and found Orest, the slave trader, waiting for me. Then he asked me to join him for lunch, and now, after a carriage ride together, I stood in front of a very *familiar* restaurant. Though I'd barely had more than a few snacks, so at least I had an alibi for allowing him to drag me here.

"Let's go right in. I have a reservation."

"You reserved a table and didn't even ask me? I could've refused, you know."

"But you didn't, did you? No harm done."

That wasn't what I meant, but I supposed it was all moot by now anyway. Still, of all places, it just *had* to be here...

"Welcome back, Sir Moulton. Your table is ready for you." The doorman bowed, gracefully opening the door for us.

Orest led the way inside, apparently familiar with the interior. I followed behind him, acknowledging the doorman on the way in.

The restaurant was adorned with a high-end carpet and decoration that distinguished itself from the tacky, "new money" look made by a mere mishmash of expensive items. The decor was refined and tasteful, maintaining a relaxing atmosphere for dining...which I had expected, considering we were standing in the most expensive restaurant in Gimul, one that even I had heard of.

I had tailored a suit for myself before, so I was thankfully able to meet the dress code.

"Right this way."

Before I knew it, Orest had exchanged a few words with the owner of the restaurant, and we were being shown to a secluded room in the back of the restaurant.

"Do please enjoy yourselves."

The owner left after briefly explaining how to order food and call for service, which finally gave me some breathing room.

Orest noticed my unease. "Did I pull you out of your element?"

"I'm just not used to this. I never come to fancy establishments like this."

"Oh? I dare say, you didn't let it show."

"Pure bravado. I didn't want to make a fool of myself."

I took a sip from a glass of water that had already been left on the table for me. "So, care to tell me why exactly you invited me to lunch?"

"To touch base. I haven't seen you since that time you came to my shop in Gaunago."

"You came all the way to Gimul for that?"

"There's a regular conference in Gimul, and I try not to miss that if I can help it."

"A conference... I think I've heard about it from Serge, Glissela the guildmaster, and Pioro from the Saionji company, if memory serves."

"So you do know of it. I believe those three also try to attend if their schedule permits. It's a conference for established current or former business owners to congregate and share ideas or propose joint ventures."

"Sounds like it's a big deal."

"Everyone there is a seasoned veteran of their trade. I merely inherited my seat from my father, so every conference is quite a learning experience for me. Would you like to attend? If you're interested, that is."

"*Me*? Oh, no, I couldn't. That sounds way out of my league."

"It's not like there are hard and fast criteria. Anyone can attend if invited by a member. Whether or not the other members condone that may be another story."

Wasn't that the important part?

"You know many of the members, and I think you'd get along just fine with those you'd be meeting for the first time. You know the owner of this place, for example."

"I had some good luck." A short while back, I struck a small deal with the owner, so we were acquainted with each other; I explained as much to Orest.

"How wonderful. He's infamous for his tough judgment of business partners. He never would have agreed to a deal without considering you worthy."

"Really?" Now that was a memo I didn't get.

I did hear later that the owner, who also owned the expensive inn that I had stayed in on my first night in Gimul with the duke's family, had recognized me as the kid who tagged along with them… I wasn't sure that the owner's decision was strictly based on our terms, but I was confident enough that our deal was mutually beneficial.

"May I ask what sort of deal it is?" Orest inquired.

"Yeah, I don't see an issue with telling you, since this isn't the only establishment I've struck a deal like this with… But it's to do with processing trash."

Wouldn't it be against etiquette to discuss such an unhygienic topic here?

"It's a private room, and I certainly don't mind. I'm interested in your venture, Ryoma."

There was no problem, then... And of course, he already knew about the trash plant. He hadn't changed one bit.

"I buy the food they would otherwise discard. Most foods have an expiration date, and once it goes bad, no one can eat it. However, there are some noticeable changes that are harmless, such as discoloration due to oxidation, or you being able to cut off the damaged part. That being said, not many establishments would want to serve food like that, especially swankier places like this one."

"True."

"I buy foods that they would otherwise have to discard at a large markdown. Out of sanitation concerns and respect for the restaurants, I promise not to resell or give away any food or dishes made from them."

For restaurants, having to throw away food was a pure loss. With me stepping in to buy them, the restaurants' financial hurt was at least mitigated. My benefit was that I could obtain foods nearing their expiration for dirt cheap.

"I used the food I buy to feed my familiar slimes and goblins, as well as to research preserves. That's more of a hobby, though. I also built a dedicated warehouse next to the trash plant that holds these foods." This deal didn't net me a profit, but greatly reduced the food budget for my many familiars.

Some were rotten or moldy and therefore inedible, but it seemed like a waste to not try to salvage what was usable. Even in Japan, this used to be something every household did when I was growing up, but some of my subordinates looked at me like I was crazy over it. One of the younger ones once told me with a rather straight face that "this isn't wartime..." Maybe I was just a gigantic cheapskate.

Wait, what the hell am I doing thinking about this at an expensive restaurant? A rush of embarrassment came over me.

At that moment, servers entered with our food, as if they had been waiting for the perfect time. They brought in a cart of dishes, which they swiftly transferred to our table. I had expected to be served in courses just because they were a fancy restaurant, but apparently not this time. Still, our table now hosted a few different appetizers in small portions and presented beautifully—a salad with fresh vegetables not obtainable to most, a rare mushroom soup, the steak entrée... Every dish exuded decadence.

As soon as the dishes were placed on our table, the servers swiftly exited.

"This restaurant is frequented by people of considerable status. Private rooms are used for business meetings both legitimate and not, so the staff are very considerate."

"I see. That's why they simply set the table with our food and left..."

Wait, did he just read my mind?!

"It's only written all over your face. Anyway, let's eat."

Very well. I couldn't waste a meal like this. He didn't have to twist my arm about it. I started with an appetizer.

"How do you like it?"

"Delicious, of course. And it's very extravagant."

The ingredients of these dishes—the fresh vegetables, for example—were specially created by magic. Those were sold at market price, which was at least ten times the price of the same vegetable when they were naturally grown and sold in season.

What's truly surprising was that the upper class, who were the target market of restaurants like these, ate food like this on a daily basis… It really was delicious.

"I'm glad you enjoyed it. Was I able to be of assistance the other day?"

"That's right! I need to thank you for that." A while back, I had asked for his help. "Thank you for helping on such short notice. It aided greatly with the security of my and my acquaintances' shops, and reduced crime levels in the city as well."

"That's wonderful. I was definitely surprised when you sent me a letter asking to buy a criminal slave."

"I'm sorry about that. The city was getting more dangerous by the day, and I felt like I had no time at all… Sorry for being so shortsighted."

"Oh, no. I think it was a very calculated and logical decision—hiring a criminal who has been made a slave as their sentence in order to improve security by gaining insight from a criminal's perspective."

I remember how I had heard about American government institutions hiring some criminals as crime prevention advisers, and thought I would give it a shot. Unfortunately, I was informed that there was legal red tape and qualifications I would have had to meet in order to purchase a criminal slave. So, Orest had interviewed one of them in my stead. The information he sent in his letter was greatly effective for me personally and for the city at large. Without them, it would have taken significantly longer to reduce the crime rate.

"I would very much like for you to owe me favors, so please reach out to me anytime if there's anything I can help you with," Orest said, with clear matter-of-factness. "So, the city has gotten safer. How have you been doing lately? I've heard you used to live in the forest. Are you adjusting to city life?"

"What are you, my dad…? Yes, I do enjoy it. My shop is doing well, and so am I, personally. Also, this may sound weird, but if it wasn't for the rise in crime in Gimul, I would not have gotten to know some people that I have."

The first that came to mind was the owner of the restaurant we were in, and the tailor who had worked on my suit, with whom I had struck a deal to provide work uniforms for my security company and the trash plant. I could safely say that I had gotten closer to other acquaintances around the city, and even those delinquent adventurers, in some way.

Time flew by as I detailed some of those examples to Orest. Before I knew it, we were halfway done with our meal.

"I've been the only one talking. I'm sorry."

"No need to apologize. I was the one who asked. And, if you remember from when we first met, I enjoy listening to others more than talking by myself."

Now that he mentioned it… There was just too much new information at the time, so this nugget must have gotten buried.

"Would you mind if I share something with you?" he added. "I would love for us to get to know each other more."

"Of course."

I could only hope that I would be able to understand Orest better, since I was never entirely sure what went through his mind.

⤙ Chapter 7 Episode 35 ⤚
Orest's Woes

"Right, allow me to be frank. As you know, I am a slave trader; I was born to parents who were also slave traders, and have enjoyed a privileged life from my youth. That being said, most people see slave trading as little more than transacting people like products on a shelf. Personally, I can profess that things aren't so simple… But it's certainly true that we put prices on people. Not many have a good impression of the profession. Because of this, I never had anyone I could call a friend when I was a child. Because of the parents of my peers, more often than not."

This I could imagine well—parents being overprotective and whatnot.

"I found myself seeking out every chance to speak to the service staff of the house, my parents' employees, and the slaves. In hindsight, I was looking for whatever substitute I could find for friends my own age. When I started, I was no doubt calculating in the back of my mind that people who worked for my parents wouldn't treat me poorly, and slaves couldn't run away from my conversations. As I got to know more and more people, I began to realize that no two of them were the same. Their race, family legacy, birthplace, work history, their nature, down to their beliefs and preferences were all so different. I genuinely enjoyed getting to know them, learning about our differences, and gaining new knowledge and outlooks. At some point, I wasn't looking for a substitute friend but wanting to know the person before me." Now, Orest met my eyes with an intent look. "I used my profession to meet many people from all walks of life. And I strongly feel like you are different from any of them. That's why I want to get to know you better. My personal curiosity was one of the reasons why I invited you to dine with me today."

Most likely because I'm from another world. "I am aware that I don't exactly fit into the parameters of normality. What are your other reasons?"

Orest gave a confident smile. "I want to form an alliance with you, Ryoma. What do you think of the slave trade?"

"What do I think of it...? I don't know, if I'm being honest. I must admit I have some resistance against the term. But the practice is legal here, and you treat your slaves well enough that I struggle to find a practical difference between enslavement and long-term employment. I also learned that slavery is a final frontier for many who have fallen to poverty. So I can't say for or against it at the moment, if that's what you're asking."

Despite my purposefully vague answer, Orest seemed even happier. "Thank you. That was more than I had hoped for. Slave trading would be much easier if all of our customers were as understanding as you. If I may vent for a bit, many customers do not understand the nature of slavery or the practices of the slave trade. That's considered an inevitability in our industry, and we'll tell any newcomer to the business the same. But," he continued, staring into my eyes, "I think that the slave trade, or slavery altogether, is outdated."

Back in modern-day Japan, I could only find legal slavery in history or fiction. It was very possible that, as this world became more modernized, they would follow the same trend.

"As you've said, Ryoma, the official enslavement contract in accordance with slavery laws is very similar to a freelance contract signed at any guild. The difference, I suppose, is that the purchaser of a slave needs to provide the slave's necessities, and they pay what they would pay as a worker's salary to the slave trader upfront. The gap between these contracts have only lessened because, with the abolishment of the old slave laws that permitted inhumane treatment of slaves, new slave laws were established along with the concept of human rights that is now seeping into society. Just to be clear, I have no intention of denouncing the concept of human rights. In fact, I believe it's an important value that all of us must keep in our minds at all times. That is precisely why I think the slave trade is outdated. The only reason why I am able to maintain my career as a slave trader at all is because slavery provides the last resort for destitute people to survive, and because the nobles who chart the course of society and value tradition but fear change consider the slave trade a part of their tradition. I couldn't help but think that, in the near future, slavery will have no place in our world... I've been thinking about how a slave trader can adapt to these changing times."

"I've heard that you began *renting* slaves, which is a more temporary and reasonable option."

"That's correct. I thought you would notice. You mentioned 'human resources' and 'agency' when I last spoke of it."

"I said that...?"

"You muttered them while you were reading my pamphlet."

"Past me let my mouth slip in front of *you*, of all people."

"When I heard that, my opinion of you skyrocketed. You have tangible knowledge about the future of slavery as I envision it. Even if you don't, I felt that you would understand my concern for the future. I know it."

Understand his concern...

At this point, I finally felt like I'd realized something new about Orest. He must have been a truly talented businessman. Not just above average or top tier, but a once-in-a-generation genius. I didn't know what kind of effort he had put in to get this far, and I might have been disrespecting him by chalking all of his work up to him being a genius. That being said, there was a real difference between a genius and a layman, a deep and cruel divide. Orest's talent allowed him to foresee a future many in this world did not. Long story short, he was too ahead of his time.

"I don't know much about the industry of slavery," I offered, "but many slave traders believe that their situation will not change for a long time. You're looking generations into the future, when your children or grandchildren would inherit the business."

"Precisely. All we can do is imagine and speculate about the future... But I can't help but think that a future of unknown change awaits us. That's why I believe we have to search for a new adaptation of slavery."

"And you arrived at a human resource agency."

"I am not married to the slave trade, but when I think of a way to best utilize our accumulated knowledge and experience, I thought it best to provide training to applicants to raise their value as an employee and introduce them to potential employers."

I admitted it was a good idea for him to use the tools he'd honed in the slavery industry. "I am concerned about the treatment of the employees. We can only imagine what future laws would bring to the table..."

Temp workers in Japan, for example, had suffered lack of work and low pay due to laws regarding the practice... It was easy for outsiders to tell them to get a full-time job, but that was easier said than done. Many became trapped in a negative spiral that was hard to get out of, and it was easy to blame the workers themselves for their predicament because they "didn't work hard enough to get a real job." At the end of the day, I was never able to give up my full-time employment, no matter how badly my company treated me. I had wondered many times if working as a temp would have made things much easier.

I used my memories to point out some concerns to Orest, and he listened so intently that I felt a physical pressure across the table. He kept me talking about what I knew about the temp work system from Japan, under the guise of a possible future I could envision, while we finished the rest of our meal, as well as a full dessert, and continued during our carriage ride all the way back to the security company.

When we were about to part, he said in a somewhat calmer manner, "Oh, I had such a wonderful time today. This is the first time I have been able to discuss the future in such detail and envision concrete possibilities."

"I thought we had fruitful conversations as well."

Orest was still hard to read, but he had helped me out a lot, so I was glad I could help him.

"If there's anything I can be of assistance for, please let me know. Slavery or otherwise."

"Thank you. I'll take you up on that." I thought my reply was inoffensive, but Orest stared at me thoughtfully. "Is something the matter?"

"Ryoma, I want to become closer to you. I really, truly do. That is why I want to give you advice, albeit unsolicited. Do you remember how I asked you if you were enjoying your life lately?"

Of course I did. And I answered honestly.

"I don't doubt that you told me the truth," he continued. "In fact, I could tell that you really treasure each day from the bottom of your heart."

I felt a bit red in the cheeks to have someone tell me this head on, but I also felt a sort of joy or relief that even others could see that I was appreciating my life.

"Many people only realize what they've had after they lose it. The significance of ordinary, day-to-day life in particular is often overlooked. But in every one of your words describing how you enjoyed your days, I felt how strongly you appreciate your life...and a strong fear of losing it."

"Fear?"

"You seemed like a man who finally grasped a treasure you've longed for years. Someone like that wouldn't want to lose their treasure again. I felt like, subconsciously, you are trying to be the *good boy* who obediently listens to everything adults tell him... You seem very happy but very confined."

I stood for a few moments, not quite understanding his meaning.

"It's not worth worrying about," he quickly said. "It was nonsense. Please forget about it."

He bid me goodbye and took his carriage away. Orest was showing more of his emotions today, and after our discussion, he did feel more straightforward and easier to read. But looking back on it now, there was still much I didn't understand about him...

❧ Chapter 7 Episode 36 ☙
Conversation of the Puppet Masters

In the capital city, the glimmering lights of noble manors and high-class establishments lit up the dark of night. The glittering cityscape had been described as "a field of fallen stars," and that "a single view was worth a thousand piles of gold."

One man stood at a window of his manor gazing out at that view. "What of our operation in Gimul?" he asked, still facing the window.

Behind the man, another wearing a well-tailored suit and an obscure mask emerged from the shadows of the room. "We managed to increase crime temporarily, but it has been dealt with more effectively than we had anticipated. With crime steadily lessening, our plan is sure to fail."

"Your concern was well grounded, after all... Ryoma Takebayashi. You had mentioned him to me, but I must admit I had underestimated him. I didn't expect him to accommodate all of the new job seekers we sent in. A brutish solution of throwing cash at the problem, but effective nonetheless. But how come there's no sign of the duke backing him up? Don't tell me the boy has enough money on his own."

"There's a chance we didn't catch the exchange, but the larger the bill, the harder it would be to hide. The goods most likely came from Ryoma Takebayashi."

The first man showed a hint of dissatisfaction. "Do you know exactly who the boy is?"

"Nothing more than previous reports. We contacted an underground guild that specializes in reconnaissance. The only points of information we received on him before the Jamils brought him out into the city is that he was a hermit in the forest, that he was born in a village within the Sea of Trees of Syrus, and that he was probably treated badly in said village."

"Is he from the underground, like you?"

"I considered the possibility, but found no evidence that he has any connection to the underground or its guilds."

"There are many factions of underground guilds, aren't there? Could one of them be trying to cover up intel on him?"

"True, the guilds are far from united. There are specialized guilds for each job like thievery, assassination, fraud, smuggling... However, I suspect one would be unable to find information on Ryoma Takebayashi because of the special nature of the Sea of Trees of Syrus, and his own abilities acquired from that special land."

"If you're sure, then we'll set aside his origin." The man turned around from the window to face the man in the mask, his eyes gleaming like ice. "Eliminate Ryoma Takebayashi at all costs."

"Are you certain...? The duke has clearly put a lot of stock in the boy. He will have something to say about it."

The man by the window scoffed. "For some time, Reinhart has been approaching our noble friends at balls to deter their involvement, which means they are taking things seriously. It's a matter of time before we're revealed. Some of our more timid comrades have turned to protect themselves, but you won't find me begging for mercy. If I was going to be sorry for it, I never would have planned it in the first place. If our time is limited, the best we can do is strike back as much as possible. The more Reinhart treasures Ryoma Takebayashi, the more pain our next operation will bring him. I do have a vendetta against him for sabotaging our operations. The boy will pay for interfering with matters beyond his understanding!" The man spoke with more and more gusto...or perhaps madness.

Seeing that the man had forsaken the possibility of retreat or surrender, the masked man gave up on trying to persuade him otherwise. "Understood. I will design the best plan to accommodate my client's wishes. That is my job, after all."

"I admire your professionalism. Let's get into details. What tricks do you have in mind?"

"If attacking Ryoma Takebayashi directly, you will need several well-trained fighters to do the job and to isolate the target before the attack. The target should be worn out as much as possible. Considering the reports on him, he would rather bring harm to himself than those close to him, which has driven him to actively sabotage our plan. Therefore, without having to interact with him directly, he is very unlikely to ignore trouble in the city or with someone close to him. If both were to happen at the same time, he would be stretched thin."

"Is all of this necessary for a mere boy?"

"I believe that is the bare minimum required for a successful operation. That boy holds powers we still don't know about."

The man by the window considered the past reports. "All right. I trust your decision. Let's go with that."

"Thank you."

"The boy has destroyed every plan we could conceive. We must take every possible precaution. I must correct myself... I keep thinking that a single child can only do so much."

"Indeed, there is only so much that regular children could do. Our target just happens to be a boy outside the scope of what is normal. I was only lucky enough to see him in person, which helped me readjust my expectations early on."

144

"Come to think of it, you used to be undercover in the guild, right?"

"We needed to set the stage for our initial plan."

"What did you see?"

"I more felt it. When I realized that our initial plan was thwarted, I used a convenient request from another client, and as a form of petty revenge, sicced some money-grubbers his way. Watching his tactics, movements, and the air about him… It's difficult to explain, but the boy is dangerous. He should not be approached directly if we can help it."

"If he makes *you* say so…"

The man in the mask was a planner, the brain or command center of the underground guild that planned crimes, prepared supplies, and gathered human resources. They were the adviser to people like the man by the window, the clients of the underground guilds. Even in those guilds, certain trust and experience are expected for those in charge of planning or executing a quest. Especially because the slightest mistake could cost the team their lives, the weight of expectation on their leader was greater than other professions. Naturally, most planners were longtime criminals who had their hands in many gigs. The masked man had been introduced to his client as a young but talented planner, and had proven his usefulness until now. Because the man highly esteemed the planner, he was all the more surprised by the masked man's confession.

"I am very much inexperienced," the planner said. "In reality, the boy has ended three of my plans already." Despite his self-deprecation, the planner sounded confident.

The client sensed a fire for revenge in his tone. "Very well… Let's get back on the topic at hand. I'll leave the details up to you. If possible, I want you to go after the president of the Morgan company.

He has aided both Ryoma Takebayashi and Reinhart. His loss would come as a blow to both of them."

"As you wish."

"And now that I'm adding provisions to the original request, how much do I owe you?"

"Let me gather the men for the job first. But this is a result of my first plan failing. A plan B. I'll have a heavy discount for the fee."

"That's fine by me, but send me the bill sooner than later. You won't be able to collect the money from me when I'm imprisoned." The man smiled. "Oh! If you're going to give me a discount, I'd like to add another task."

"Go ahead."

"If I... You need to..." the man quietly explained.

"I can take that as a request, but are you sure? It may only hurt you in the end, and if you end up in that situation, there would be no way to cancel or change the plan."

"That's fine. I'll spend as much money as it takes to pay back Reinhart and the Jamils. Here, take this too." The man took an ornately designed sword off of the wall and presented it to the masked man. "A jeweled sword of orichalcum that my great-grandparents obtained. You could melt it down and still fetch a good price for it."

"It must be a very valuable piece... This will pay for Ryoma Takebayashi's elimination and your additional provisions."

"If you'll accept it, that's fine with me. Saves me the time to gather the cash."

A deal was struck.

As soon as the masked man took the sword, he vanished into the shadows. The man left behind returned to gazing out the window with a sinister grin on his face.

⇜ Chapter 7 Episode 37 ⇝
Activity in the Capital

While Ryoma worked at his own pace in Gimul, Duke Reinhart, his wife Elise, and their daughter Eliaria could be found in the royal palace—the core of the kingdom and symbol of the king's influence. A guide led them through ornately decorated hallways, befitting the royal architecture. After passing several doors they eventually came to a particularly large and heavyset one, guarded by two knights each on either side. Their guide spoke to the knights, and several of the knights proceeded to question, then pat down the trio. Once they were permitted to enter, the door made an artificial mechanical noise as it opened by itself.

"It's a magical item."

"Oh? Don't you remember the last time you were here, Elia?"

"No, mother. Has this always been in the palace? I don't recall seeing it on prior visits here."

"This is the royal gate. It's been here for hundreds of years, long before any of us. The door separates the most important sector of the already important palace, the private space of the royal family. Everyone needs to go through the security procedure we just did, and the door won't open until a knight uses a different magical item to signal someone else in another room who triggers the door to open."

"I didn't realize it was so complex."

"No need to explain how a piece of security works to every guest, I suppose. Besides, you were very little when you were last here, Elia. It's no wonder you don't remember. What's important, Elia, is that we are entering the private quarters of the royal family. You won't know who we'll run into. Make sure you are employing perfect etiquette. Be very careful."

"Yes, father." Elia answered nervously and straightened her posture.

Reinhart nodded in approval, and stared ahead of the open door. Soon, the three began following the guide again, eventually coming to another door which the guide called into.

"Your Majesty, the Jamils have arrived."

"Enter," a brisk growl answered.

The guide swiftly stepped aside, and Reinhart stood before the door with Elise behind him. Only Elia followed behind her parents, and the three slowly entered through the open door. According to proper etiquette, they took three steps after Elia completely entered the room before kneeling and bowing. Just as Reinhart attempted to speak, a voice shattered the solemn air.

"Go on, imbeciles. Get on your feet and come sit down."

Reinhart raised his head and gave the speaker a dirty look, more out of exasperation than anger. "Erias, have you no tact?"

"Hmph! As if these stuffy rituals would do me any favors! It's a waste of time, and what need is there for formalities between us? I play king well enough in public, so do let me relax in the comfort of my room."

"There has to be some bare minimum of decorum. I even brought my daughter with me—"

"Yes! So happy to see you, Elia. My, how you've grown!" Erias called joyfully.

"Y-Yes, Your Majesty…"

"What's this?! You used to call me 'uncle'!"

"Th-That was when I was much younger… I am twelve already. I couldn't possibly—"

"I don't mind! No one else is here! You can *always* call me uncle."

"But…"

"Well, you have to sit on the couch first. Come, sit. Don't stay on your knees like that. You can even sit on my lap, like when you were little…" Erias's attitude had even his dear niece taken aback.

Reinhart, who was attempting to rescue his daughter from his best friend, noticed something, shuddered, and covered his ears.

"Enough!" Elise snapped at the excessively brazen king.

■　■　■

Ten minutes later, Elia sat on the couch with her parents on either side, with Erias sprawled across from them, looking rather downhearted. Erias wore a casual outfit crafted from the best materials in the country over his toned body and characteristically full mustache. He would have carried considerable regality and dignity with a little bit of poise, but none could be found at the moment. This was the one and only Erias De Rifall, Reinhart's best friend, Elise's older brother, Elia's uncle and godfather, and the king of Rifall Kingdom where Ryoma lived.

"Can't you get up already? We are your guests," Elise said.

"You're not my guests, you're family."

"Elia started in the academy this year. She'll be expected to act appropriately in certain situations. I brought her here so she can practice her etiquette as much as possible, only for her king to act like this…"

"When I relax, I *relax*! When I act kingly, I act kingly. I know where to draw the line."

"You always were great at making excuses."

"Cut me some slack. It's not easy to be the king. These past few years have been especially tough, what with the monsters becoming more active all over the country... Want to take over the throne, Reinhart?"

"No. And that's not an offer you should be making lightly."

"It's so stressful... I don't want to work anymore."

"Even so, who hosts their guests lying down on the couch?"

"Your king."

"You are very stubborn in your laziness today."

"Yes, I am. Why don't you tell me why you're here? Let's get the boring stuff over with." Erias looked at the three somberly, albeit still on his side.

Reinhart ignored the discordant contrast in the king's serious expression and unserious posture. "Bring us our parcel, please." He took a small box from the guide who had been standing aside, and passed it on to Erias.

"Let me see..." The king chuckled as if he had been given a toy as he lifted his upper body with his arm. "A pearl necklace. Each of them are large, with uniform color and shape. Spectacular. You won't find this anywhere in our country, and you'd be hard pressed to find it even where pearls are harvested. Where did you get this? Why bring it to me?"

"I did promise my source I wouldn't tell. I promise it's not smuggled or illegal. Keep it. As a gift for Her Majesty. If you want more, I can bring you more."

The king smiled. "Very well. The queen's been looking for nice pieces for the upcoming balls. I'll have her wear it to them. I'll give the 'royal stamp of approval' for all pearls handled by you."

Elia looked at her uncle curiously. "Uncle, you understood father's intention from that gift alone?"

"I made an educated guess considering the current state of his territory...and we've known each other for so long. I've heard that some nobles are sabotaging things in your land, and that your parents have been showing up to parties, which they used to avoid at all cost. He brings a necklace to me now, and tells me he can get more. I can assume your father is trying to strengthen his influence and connections in high society in exchange for these pearls. That means Reinhart and Elise are here to ask me to make those dealings easier for them. They also understand what I can and would do very well. They wouldn't request anything I couldn't provide. Even if their request is a big one, I was sure they'd make it worth my while." He gave them a mischievous grin.

Elia looked back and forth between her parents, who seemed to share an expression. She felt a swell of adoration for the strong trust they shared with the king.

"Anything else I can do for you?" the king asked.

"That's plenty. There's no point if we rely too much on you, anyway."

"Thought so. If there's nothing else you wanted to talk about, I have something in mind."

"What is it?" Elise prompted.

"Ryoma Takebayashi."

Elia showed the largest reaction of the three. She kept silent, but her expression betrayed the surprise of hearing a familiar name. Reinhart and Elise shared an understanding look shortly after.

"So you *have* heard about him," Elise said.

"The rumors of crime in your territory had reached me. If it was any other territory, I might not have paid it any heed, but when my dear friend, sister, and niece are there... I couldn't help but send an informant into the city who reports to me regularly."

"That's how you heard of Ryoma."

"He's putting on quite the show. Apparently, all rumors nowadays end up being about young Ryoma, somehow. By complete coincidence, my informant had found a job at Ryoma's laundry shop to earn coin for his travel. In his latest report, he said he now served as the boy's bodyguard."

"Your man is that close to him?" Reinhart asked, thinking of the men and women he had sent to Ryoma.

"Funny enough, the boy *knows* he works for me, and keeps him close anyway."

Reinhart's jaw dropped. "What did you say?" he asked, disbelieving his ears.

Erias summarized how Hudom became Ryoma's bodyguard.

"So Ryoma vetoed the others?"

"Long story short. I'm sure you'll hear the details from your employees soon. Even though he knew my informant wouldn't harm him, it takes some courage to keep a spy from an unknown source by his side. What's more, he sent me detailed information about Gimul by sharing it all in front of my informant."

"What is Ryoma thinking..." Elia muttered, to her parents' silent agreement.

"It's not a bad move. As the king, I naturally stand above any noble that may be interfering with your territory, and lean towards its favor. He understood this much and gave me information. Trying to play the king... If I had been more of an elitist... Well, it *would* come across as patriotic, actively cooperating with the king's informant. It also wouldn't make sense to create unnecessary rifts. He thought all of this through... Anyway, I like his guts! Why didn't you tell me about this fun kid sooner?!"

"Because I knew you'd say that," Elise said.

"He's a good kid, but he sometimes does things out of the blue..."

Reinhart and Elise tried to imagine a meeting between Ryoma and the king, and failed. All they knew was that the meeting would not end well.

"Nothing good would come of meeting the kid? Is that all?"

"What else is there? I can't even count how many times you roped me into your whims."

"Fine... I want to meet him, but I don't have the time, anyway. But let me tell you this: hold his reins tight." Erias no longer carried any playful air. "I'm not the only one who caught wind of the name Ryoma Takebayashi and got a glimpse of his powers. Anyone in a decent circle, noble or commoner, would have heard by now. If you mean to protect him, keep him within arm's reach. The kid isn't exactly a straight arrow. I'm sure he means well for your house and Gimul at large, but he has more initiative and drive than most adults; his abilities give him great influence. Let's say the kid goes rogue and something goes wrong. If he's the only one who suffers for it, he deserves it. I don't wish his actions to negatively affect you, but I can look past it if your family is the only one affected. But, worse comes to worst, if the boy becomes a threat to the country, I will not tolerate it. I would be forced...to execute him," Erias declared with unwavering resolve and kingly aura.

Reinhart and Elise hardened at his change of tone.

"It will be okay," Elia calmly interjected, garnering the eyes of the adults. "Oh... I interrupted you uncle, I'm so sorry."

"No matter. Can you tell me why you think it will be all right?"

"I was thinking out loud..." Elia spoke, choosing her words. "Ryoma is a strange person. He starts bizarre projects, and he knows a lot of things but lacks common sense, sometimes. But Ryoma is a kind person. He can be caring in a strange or excessive way... At the very least, Ryoma always made sure that we and other people were safe, the best he could. Besides, Ryoma knows a lot of things we don't, and he's great at magic but strong even without it. Still, he never boasted about his abilities or tried to manipulate others by using them. He always tried to help other people through his knowledge and abilities."

"Indeed, that matches what I hear from my reports," Erias confirmed.

"Uncle, I know I have not met nearly as many people as you, or father, or mother have. But, I still met many new people as I started at the academy this year. I learned the hard way that some people, rich or poor, want to push their twisted logic, try to control others by force or their status alone, look down on others just because they were better at some minor thing... People who could barely hold a conversation. Ryoma isn't like them. He sometimes seemed to lack common sense, but only because he had been a recluse for so long. He would always listen to criticism, and admitted fault when he had some. Ryoma is someone I can count on to reach a common understanding on anything. I heard that he had always consulted father or another adult before taking action. Isn't that right, father? Mother?"

"That's true."

"He did ask this time. More of an ask for forgiveness, but still."

"See! And Ryoma always writes that he enjoys living every day because people help him. I can't imagine him trying to harm or even inconvenience others on purpose. So… What I'm trying to say is…" Elia failed to find more words, but kept stammering, becoming increasingly desperate to get her point across.

Her uncle burst into laughter. "I see, I see…"

"Uncle?"

"It's all right. I get your point, Elia."

"Did you really?"

"If my dear niece is so sure of it… Do you agree with her, Reinhart? Elise?"

The pair shared a look.

"Yes. We'll keep an eye on him. Don't worry."

"Elia said it all."

"Then I'll trust you with him. He'll get even more attention, good and bad, from here on out. Don't let some noble steal him from under your nose," Erias said as he sat up. He patted Elia's head. "I didn't think you'd protect him so fervently, Elia. Do you trust him that much?"

"What? Yes, of course… Why do you ask, uncle?"

"Hm… I do want to meet Ryoma Takebayashi…so I can sock that kid in the face."

"Uncle?! Where is this coming from?!"

"Oh, never mind it. Why don't we play a game? I have plenty of card games and board games."

"Don't change the subject, uncle!"

"That's enough business for the day! Let's play!"

The three were forced to play a few board games with the king before returning to their house in the capital.

The king, who managed to dodge Elia's persecution, mused aloud to a thick stack of paperwork once he was alone. "Reinhart has all but won the battle… But his enemy won't stand idly by in the meantime, especially if it's who I think he is... Seeing their roundabout tactics, I doubt they'll go after Eliaria and her family directly... But what about Reinbach? That would be suicide. The most likely to suffer a direct attack are those close to Reinhart. I would expect them to direct their attention to Ryoma making such a show... How will he overcome that? He's very likely to survive an attack, if I'm right about him... If he's that good a fighter, I need to take him by surprise to get *my* hit in... Could I slam him with a dropkick from the throne when he first enters and kneels? Perhaps..." Somehow, the king began seriously plotting how to strike Ryoma.

⇜ Chapter 7 Episode 38 ⇝
At the Ball

A week passed after Eliaria and her parents met King Erias in his quarters. The king was hosting a grand ball in the largest room of the palace. The ballroom was split into six different levels, the highest level occupied by the king and the royal family, the dukes and their families below them, then the marquis' families below them, then the counts, viscounts, and barons. It was customary for those of lower rank to arrive earlier, although everyone was expected to be there before the official commencement of the ball.

Most attendees had arrived by now and were waiting for the ball to start. They had already begun conversing with each other, commencing the verbal jousting that was ever prevalent in noble gatherings… The noble children who started the academy this year, however, were the real stars of this particular ball. With the expectation to become integral members of the government, they were gathered here (whether they knew it or not) to be celebrated and accessed. With many of the noble parents watching over their children like hawks, some out of genuine concern and others to ensure immaculate etiquette, and others already sussing out potential matches for their children to marry, the ballroom was filled with a peculiar tension. If Ryoma had been there, he would have described it as a terribly intimidating parent observation day at school.

Another child and their parents arrived at the ball. A bell announced their entrance, drawing the attention of the participants. After a beat, an attendant by the entrance declared, "Announcing the duke Reinhart Jamil, the duchess Elise Jamil, and Lady Eliaria Jamil!"

Because of how the ballroom was structured, the family was in full view of the crowd, but they moved breezily and elegantly. Each of their outfits was accented by large pearls. Their appearance and poise caused some murmuring among the other participants.

"The Jamils are on a whole different level from us."

"Lady Eliaria just started at the academy this year. Look how confidently she walks."

"That's Duke Jamil? He's so handsome... Unlike father."

"Look at Duchess Elise in her crimson dress, and Lady Eliaria's brilliant blue... They're both gorgeous. And that jewelry."

"Duke Reinhart's lapel, and the ladies' earrings all have such large pearls... The Jamils are spectacular as always."

"Their clothes are, of course, excellently made, but they are tastefully reserved enough to make the pearls pop and keep the look classy overall. Such a refreshing sight compared to the tacky, new money nobles down there."

"I want those earrings too, father."

"One of *those*? Do you know how much even *one* pearl costs...?"

"Any woman would be interested in pearls as beautiful as those. Don't you agree, dear?"

"Just call for the jeweler tomorrow and get one."

"Don't you understand what those pearls are worth?"

"It's just a jewel. They'll have it at the store."

Voices rippled behind the Jamils as they elegantly passed the parted crowd.

The ball was set up as a buffet, and the participants were allowed to roam and mingle, but no one spoke to the Jamils at the moment. Unwritten etiquette prevented anyone from directly speaking to those of a higher status. If someone wanted to converse with those of higher rank, they had to wait until they were spoken to, or ask for someone with a closer relationship to introduce them. Stopping them mid-entrance was out of the question.

The Jamils reached their designated position without interruptions, and began greeting the nobles they knew, starting with other dukes and duchesses and working their way down.

"I'm sorry to interrupt. Are you Count Bernard?"

"Duke. What a pleasant surprise."

"Please be at ease. I've been meaning to thank you."

"Thank me?" Bernard searched his memory for any reason to be thanked by the duke, but none came to mind.

"I also need to thank your friends... Is Count Sandrick in attendance today?"

"I haven't seen the count tonight... He must have much on his mind, lately."

"Oh, yes. I'm sure he's quite busy at the moment. How about the viscounts Fargatton, Danielton, and Anatoma? Are they down there?"

"I'm not sure."

"I see... Well, I have quite a few thanks to give. Are you sure you don't know what I'm thanking you for?"

Bernard, of course, realized that Reinhart was not here to give genuine thanks. The duke continued pressuring the count with a beaming smile.

"How strange. It's been a great help that so many people have been sent from your land when our new city quarters are in construction. I'm talking about a few hundred people. You haven't noticed that large of a population leaving?"

Reinhart hadn't raised his voice in the slightest. But the duke had walked his way down to the counts just to talk to Bernard. This left those around them, simply rather curious or waiting to sneak in an introduction to the duke, hanging on every word of their conversation. This led to an outburst of hushed murmurs.

"What is he talking about? Hundreds of people?"

"That's like an entire village. Even for farmers going out for day labor, that's too many."

"If they were sent to aid the duke, there's nothing wrong with the emigration... But the count says he knows nothing about it. What does this mean, runaway citizens?"

"The fact that the count didn't notice is a bigger problem than their reason for leaving. How did he not know? How is he managing his territory?"

"If they fled his land, then why? I hadn't heard of any issues with the count's finances or treatment of the people... Maybe things aren't as they seem, under the surface."

The speculation of the crowd was only worsened for Bernard by them hearing bits and pieces of Reinhart's statements. Some nobles who were overhearing had begun piecing things together.

"He must be feigning ignorance because he knows everything."

"What would be the point of doing that?"

"He must have considered it worse to admit he knew."

"Oh? Do you know something we don't?"

"It's something I heard the other day... Remember the rumor that Gimul was becoming less safe?"

"Yes... I don't fault Duke Reinhart too much, as he's still young."

"Rumor has it, other houses orchestrated the crime in the city. Something about multiple houses plotting against him, discarding the troublesome residents of their cities in Gimul. I even heard they hired members of the underground guilds."

"My! Come to think of it, the stories about Gimul sounded like someone was spreading them on purpose."

"Underground guilds... How dreadful. But that's why the count..."

A new speculation rippled through the crowd of nobles, and people began to tactfully distance themselves from Bernard. No one wanted to align themselves with a noble that antagonized the duke for fear of Reinhart retaliating. Noticing his growing isolation, Bernard struggled to find a way out under a mask of calm pleasantry.

"Well, tonight's a party," said Reinhart. "Let's save this discussion for another time. Excuse me."

In a split second, shock, joy, and mockery for Reinhart whirled in Bernard's mind. "Thank you for taking your time to speak with me." The count bowed deeply, having regained some calmness on the inside to match his exterior that did not betray a shred of the tumultuous undertones of their exchange.

Reinhart continued to make his rounds, his wife and daughter in tow.

"Count Fatoma. It's been too long."

"Oh! How wonderful to see you, Duke Jamil."

"This brings me back to our school days. I'd love to introduce you to my wife and daughter."

"I would be honored!"

"Wonderful. Elia, this is Count Fatoma, an upperclassman from my academy days."

"Porco Fatoma. It's a pleasure to meet you, mademoiselle."

"Eliaria Jamil. The pleasure is all mine. My father has told me much about you."

After some small talk with Fatoma, Elia gestured to a pair of families.

"Mother, do you see over there?"

"Oh? Yes, let's join them."

"Excuse me. Count Wildan, Baron Clifford… And your families, I presume."

They met up with Michelle and Riela's parents.

"Duke Jamil! Thank you for sparing your time for someone like me."

"Please, Baron. No need to be too formal. Your daughters have been very kind to mine, I hear."

"My daughter Riela is lucky to have Lady Eliaria as her classmate."

"The same goes for my daughter Michelle. I was worried about her eccentricities, but she tells me that Lady Eliaria has helped her get along with the rest of her class as well."

"I owe you both my thanks. I hear your daughters are both excellent students, and I hope our daughters can continue their friendship. Same for us parents, of course."

"Thank you," the count and baron said in unison.

Once the parents were through with their greetings, every family member was formally introduced to each other before they engaged in small talk.

After some time, the ball officially began, announced by a few rings of a bell by an attendant in the corner of the room. This prompted the nobles, including the Jamils, to return to their respective areas of the ballroom. After waiting for the participants to take their places, the attendant kneeled by the bell. On his cue, the participants followed suit, facing the royal family's section.

From the corner of the highest area of the ballroom, the king and queen entered from a door hidden behind a thick curtain, walking with dignity and their arms interlocked.

They took their seats and the king announced, "Raise your heads." The participants obliged, still kneeling. "From the bottom of my heart, I am joyful that another year has passed in peace, and that I am able to meet the young men and women who are the future of the country. That's enough of the formalities. I don't wish to bore the young among you...nor myself. Let us drink and be merry. Raise your glasses!" At this command, drinks were dispersed. After every participant seemed to have a glass in hand, the king declared. "To the bright future of our great nation and the young spirits who will lead it!"

The guests raised their glasses and drank from them, officially commencing the ball; it had begun.

"Let's go, Elia."

"Yes, father."

The Jamils returned their glasses to a server's tray and headed directly towards the king and queen. Of course, their every step drew the attention of nearby guests. Even the less observant among them noticed the pearl necklace hanging on the queen's neck. They were already aware that the Jamils all wore pearl jewelry. The suspicions of the ladies who showed interest in the pearls (and their husbands and fathers by proxy) were confirmed by the queen's thanks directed to the duke. This single interaction guaranteed that nobles would come crawling to the Jamils for those pearls. In exchange, they would further expand their influence.

There were some nobles who disliked that outcome: Count Bernard, for example. The moment he averted his eyes from the interaction that showed clear closeness between the royal couple and Reinhart, Bernard spotted the viscounts Fargatton and Danielton. The two other lords who had sent their residents to Gimul were whispering to each other, faces drained of color. The count suspected they were all thinking the same thing.

"Viscount Fargatton. Viscount Danielton."

"C-Count Bernard!"

"Thank you for—"

"There's no time for pleasantries. You were discussing *the matter at hand*?"

"Uh, well, not entirely unrelated, I suppose…"

Bernard's irritation grew at Danielton muddling his words, but he couldn't raise his voice during a ball. Bernard repeated himself in hushed frustration.

Fargatton answered instead. "Everyone is discussing our ill repute tonight."

"Who do you mean by *our*?"

"We who are involved in *the matter at hand*, Count."

Bernard listened to the whispers all around them.

"Have you heard? Viscount Fargatton isn't as *faithful* as he seems."

"Speaking of debt, I hear Viscount Danielton is up to his neck in it."

"My son is a tax collector, and he told me Baron Reefled has avoided his fair share."

"Yes, I've heard that Viscount Sergil uses his power and money to engage in all sorts of debauchery."

"I was told Count Sandrick has a trading company he treats *very* well."

"And Baron Geromon spends his nights in the red-light district."

All Bernard could hear were whispers tarnishing the reputation of the members of the conspiracy, including himself. Upon a closer listen, he could hear everything from the most minuscule secret they hid out of embarrassment to the details of their most sinister illegal activities.

"What is happening? You haven't heard from him?"

"Not a word. But it seems certain that someone is spreading our secrets."

"Even then, the rumors are starting everywhere... Like they're competing to slander us."

Bernard stood aghast as he realized his predicament. The nobles racing to smear their names was strange in itself, but it was stranger yet to hear them do it so openly. Nobles usually conversed in subtext, composing their speech as vaguely as possible to avoid being held responsible for claims. Of course, the vagueness varied on a case-by-case basis. Ordinarily, speaking ill of another noble family in a public setting like this could be taken as slanderous. Even if the rumors were true, it wouldn't bode well for the noble who dared to voice their opinion directly.

There was an exception to this rule; the atmosphere of the ball told Bernard that this was an exceptional circumstance. When a house was caught in a scandal, it was fair game to openly insult them. Even if the comment were drastic, the worst that could happen was a slap on the wrist. There was an unspoken rule where scandalous nobles lost their privilege to be respected. And once a noble's name was smeared, they were powerless. They would survive the scandal physically, but their noble pride would not. He felt the color drain from his face, knowing he would never prosper in high society.

Bernard could not deny that he and his compatriots were being treated as the walking dead of high society. The other nobles looked at them differently. Duke Jamil had orchestrated it all. Without realizing, they had been trapped in a sinking cage.

Bernard's hands had begun to shake when the king spoke and excitement rippled through the ball. The count had not heard the king speak, but quickly caught on as the crowd reverberated: "The king gave his stamp of approval for the pearls given to him by Duke Jamil." This would further increase the value of any pearl handled by the duke, and with it his influence in the country.

Count Bernard stood hopeless. He was ready to forsake all pretense and do everything it took to protect what sliver of reputation he could scavenge. The only tactic that came to mind was to grovel at the feet of every noble and beg their forgiveness. Pathetic excuses rushed through his mind. Finally, the count absentmindedly looked up from the ground, and happened to meet the eyes of the duke.

Reinhart was smiling at him. No words were exchanged, but Bernard understood well that the duke had foregone persecuting him earlier because he was already mated.

Throughout the ball, Count Bernard could be found standing as still and quiet as a statue. He spoke to no one, and no one spoke to him.

Later, the scandals of the count and his compatriots were officially brought to light, briefly amusing high society with talks of revocation, but that was all. Soon, none of them ever even broached the topic of conversation among nobles.

⤚ Extra Story ⤙
The Meeting of the Gods and the Heirloom Sword

One day, in the divine realm of the fantasy world Seilfall, Gain had called the other gods to congregate around a roundtable.

"What's the emergency, Gain? Serelipta hasn't finished serving his punishment," Kiriluel, the goddess of war, protested.

"I don't mind getting a break, but I'm curious why you called us all in. You could have sent a message for most things."

Gain produced a long, black box from thin air. All gods but Gain, Kufo, and Lulutia stared at it with apprehension.

"What is that thing…? And where'd you get it?" asked Tekun, the god of wine.

Wilieris, the goddess of the earth, visibly raised her guard. "Such an ominous… No, sinister aura…"

Fernobelia, the goddess of academia, was the first to guess the contents and origin of the box. "Gain, Kufo, and Lulutia… You three made contact with a god on Earth, didn't you? A low-ranking one at that."

"Bingo," Gain said.

"The box gave it away. It's sealed, but the power used for it feels different from any of us. Considering how often you went to Earth, the natural conclusion is that the seal was made by an Earth god. What's more, the seal is fraying. Any of us would have made a better seal, and most Earth gods would have done an even better job, since the majority are more powerful than us. Therefore, the one who

169

made this seal was an Earth god, but one lower enough in rank to have less power than us."

"Mm. Thanks for the walk-through. You're correct," said Gain.

He, along with Kufo and Lulutia, explained what happened in Earth's divine realm: about the current state of it, the Old God or Nameless One who had been sending magic over to Seilfall, and about the box before them.

"Hm…" Grimp, the god of agriculture, grunted. "I, fer one, gots a whole lotta questions. Like that 'nameless one' or whatever an' wot 'e wants, or how they be copin' with things in their own divine realm, but may as well start with what's in the box thar."

The other gods showed signs of agreement.

"So this box contains the final pair of swords made by Ryoma's father, yes?"

"Mm. I want Tekun to take a look at it first."

"Thought you'd never ask. Put it here." Tekun, the god of skill and handiwork, took the box and extracted the longer of the swords with uncharacteristic care.

"Well, I'll be…"

The sword, drawn from its protective white sheath, gleamed with an entrancing beauty that drew in and maddened those who beheld it. Tekun studied the blade from all angles for a minute. "Impressive. Only one special material of note, but…he must have researched and drilled everything into his memory, from the required amount of hammering, the temperature of the metal, fire, water… It was perfectly balanced, if that makes sense. You probably couldn't find many katanas crafted better than this."

"Special enuff ta git yer seal of approval, eh, Tekun. So what *is* this 'special material' yer on about?" Grimp asked.

"Right… It's the soul of its maker," Tekun said with audible disappointment. The other gods' expression sank. "Ryoma's dad was, undoubtedly, one of the best sword makers that ever lived. Even then, his passion kept burning and he always strove for better techniques. That's how he made this… He used the sword that was already at the best durability, cut, and shape it could as the foundation to pour all of his soul and power into. I get the gist of that part, but you know better than I do, Fernobelia." Tekun slid the box and the short sword within it towards the center of the table.

Fernobelia took it silently, and drew it from its sheath before studying it as Tekun did. "I see… It is similar to a sacrificial rite. He must have done it subconsciously, but a powerful thought awakened the magic within him, grinding down his soul in the process, skyrocketing the sword's quality as if by a curse. It allures people because the katana is treated as a work of art as well. It's like a byproduct. I hear the ideal katana remains straight, sharp, and unbroken. Ryoma's father must have given all of his essence to these two blades to make them the epitome of that ideal. In addition to the sharpness found in many masterfully forged swords, it contains powers that you could call Indestructible and All-Slice."

"What's that supposed to mean?" Serelipta chimed in. "It won't break and it'll cut anything?"

"More or less. An indestructible sword would never so much as chip no matter how poorly it's handled, and it'll never rust even if it was left to the elements for years. All-Slice means that, in addition to being very sharp, it can cut monsters in spirit form like the undead, and even magic spells. If the right person wields it, I wouldn't be surprised if it could cut gods like us."

"Dang! A weapon wot kin damage a god? That's fodder fer a real legend!"

"It just might get one. Long story short, the sword is incredibly powerful, especially for it being man-made. No matter the nature of his craft, I will praise its maker."

Not even Gain had expected the swords to be so powerful. Even gods rarely saw humans who perfected their craft to this level. "Hrm… Then what should we do with these swords? The gods of Earth wanted Ryoma to have them, since they belonged to him. They left the timing up to us, so we have the choice to not give it to him."

"I think I do want to send them to him. They're his father's keepsakes, after all."

"I agree with Kufo."

"Cain't think of a better human ta give 'er to."

"We don't have a reason to give them to any other human. My concern lies with sending something this dangerous down to the human realm."

"Well… I don't really want to keep something that can *cut a god* anywhere near me. Isn't it safer down there than keeping it up here? There's plenty of monsters to use them against, aren't there?"

"Well, as powerful as it might be, it's just a sword. It's simply a sword that became enchanted as a result of the maker pursuing the ultimate blade. Nonetheless, it's dangerous. We shouldn't make our decision lightly. Even if we are going to send them down, we should do so carefully. We should keep it under a tight seal in the divine realm until we reach our decision."

"Then I'll craft new sheaves, well, everything but the blades, to keep them sealed. We need a proper seal no matter what we do with them, don't we?"

"Can you do that for us, Tekun?"

"My idea. I'll do it."

"Then we'll leave the sealing to you. Tekun will hold on to the swords for the time being, and we will discuss what to do with them afterwards. I would like each of us to consider our options as you keep an eye on Ryoma. We'll take a vote down the road."

"Let's go!"

"Gah! Noooooooooo…!"

The meeting of the gods had concluded, and Serelipta's scream faded into nothingness.

✎ Afterword ✎

Roy here, author of *By the Grace of the Gods*! Thank you for reading Volume 11! It's been about a whole year since Volume 10, so thank you so much for your patience!

It's already the eighth year of my writing career, which naturally also means I've gotten that much older since I started; I'm starting to really *feel* the importance of taking care of my health... Stay healthy out there.

Working with his trusty reinforcements, Ryoma sees the fruits of his labor all around the city. Meanwhile, the duke is working to keep his enemies at bay or eliminate them altogether. At the same time, there is a suspicious shadow lurking around Ryoma, and the nobles in the capital will not be eliminated from high society without a fight...

With one unexpected challenge on the horizon, Ryoma learns to trust his friends and enjoy every day he has. Will he regain a truly peaceful life? What will he feel and think in the process?

We saw some significant movement in the big picture in Volume 11. I hope you enjoyed it, and that you're looking forward to what's to come in Volume 12.

In Another World With My Smartphone

25

Patora Fuyuhara

illustration・Eiji Usatsuka

VOLUME 25
ON SALE
JANUARY 2023!

Yuri Kitayama
Illustrator • Riv

OMNIBUS 8
ON SALE
JANUARY 2023!

Seirei Gensouki:
Spirit Chronicles

THE
FARAWAY
PALADIN

The Torch Port Ensemble

MANGA
OMNIBUS 4
ON SALE
NOW

NOVEL
VOLUME 4
ON SALE
NOW

Kanata Yanagino
Illustrations by: Kususaga Rin

An **ARCHDEMON'S DILEMMA:** HOW TO **LOVE YOUR ELF BRIDE**

13

FUMINORI TESHIMA

ILL. COMTA

VOLUME 13
ON SALE NOW!

AUTHOR: DOUFU MAYOI
ILLUSTRATIONS BY: KUROGIN (DIGS)

NOVEL + MANGA
AVAILABLE FROM ALL
MAJOR EBOOK STORES!

BLACK
SUMMONER

VII

VOL. 7
ON SALE NOW!

Tearmoon Empire

Nozomu Mochitsuki
Illustrator: **Gilse**

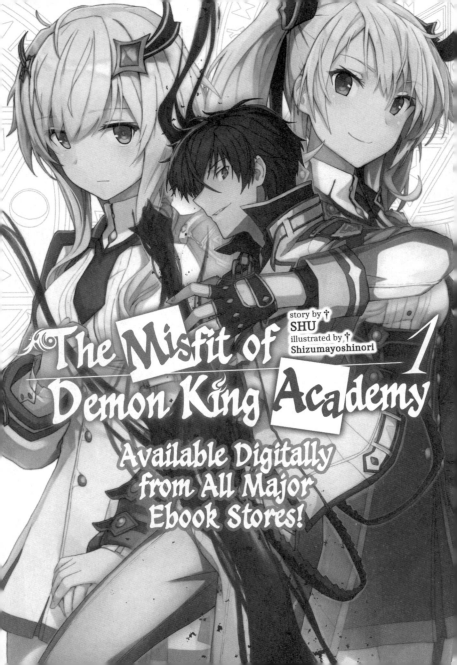

story by †
SHU
illustrated by †
Shizumayoshinori

1

The Misfit of
Demon King Academy

Available Digitally
from All Major
Ebook Stores!

Tamamaru

Illustrator Kinta

My Quiet
BLACKSMITH
Life in Another World

Volumes 1-3
Available from All
Major Ebook Stores!

Available from All
Major Ebook Stores!
The world's
longest-running sci-fi
epic, now rebooted
and in English!
PERRY RHODAN
NEO
Various Authors
Art: toi8

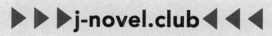

J-Novel Club Lineup

Latest Ebook Releases Series List

The Apothecary Diaries
An Archdemon's Dilemma: How to Love Your Elf Bride*
Arifureta: From Commonplace to World's Strongest
Ascendance of a Bookworm*
Backstabbed in a Backwater Dungeon
Bibliophile Princess*
Black Summoner*
By the Grace of the Gods
Campfire Cooking in Another World with My Absurd Skill*
Chillin' in Another World with Level 2 Super Cheat Powers
The Conqueror from a Dying Kingdom
Cooking with Wild Game*
D-Genesis: Three Years after the Dungeons Appeared
Dahlia in Bloom: Crafting a Fresh Start with Magical Tools
Death's Daughter and the Ebony Blade
Demon Lord, Retry!*
Der Werwolf: The Annals of Veight*
Did I Seriously Just Get Reincarnated as My Gag Character?!*
Doll-Kara**
Dragon Daddy Diaries: A Girl Grows to Greatness
Dungeon Busters
DUNGEON DIVE: Aim for the Deepest Level
Endo and Kobayashi Live! The Latest on Tsundere Villainess Lieselotte
Fantasy Inbound
The Faraway Paladin*
Forget Being the Villainess, I Want to Be an Adventurer!
Formerly, the Fallen Daughter of the Duke
Full Metal Panic!
Full Clearing Another World under a Goddess with Zero Believers*
Fushi no Kami: Rebuilding Civilization Starts With a Village*
The Great Cleric
The Greatest Magicmaster's Retirement Plan

Grimgar of Fantasy and Ash
Gushing over Magical Girls**
Hell Mode
Holmes of Kyoto
Housekeeping Mage from Another World: Making Your Adventures Feel Like Home!*
How a Realist Hero Rebuilt the Kingdom*
How NOT to Summon a Demon Lord
I Shall Survive Using Potions!*
The Ideal Sponger Life
In Another World With My Smartphone
Infinite Dendrogram*
Invaders of the Rokujouma!?
Isekai Tensei: Recruited to Another World*
John Sinclair: Demon Hunter
A Late-Start Tamer's Laid-Back Life
Lazy Dungeon Master
Maddrax
The Magic in this Other World is Too Far Behind!*
The Magician Who Rose From Failure
Marginal Operation**
Min-Maxing My TRPG Build in Another World
The Misfit of Demon King Academy
Monster Tamer
My Daughter Left the Nest and Returned an S-Rank Adventurer
My Friend's Little Sister Has It In for Me!
My Quiet Blacksmith Life in Another World
My Stepmom's Daughter Is My Ex
My Instant Death Ability is So Overpowered, No One in This Other World Stands a Chance Against Me!*
My Next Life as a Villainess: All Routes Lead to Doom!
Now I'm a Demon Lord! Happily Ever After with Monster Girls in My Dungeon
Otherside Picnic
Oversummoned, Overpowered, and Over It!*
Perry Rhodan NEO

Prison Life is Easy for a Villainess
Private Tutor to the Duke's Daughter
Re:RE — Reincarnation Execution
Reborn to Master the Blade: From Hero-King to Extraordinary Squire ♀*
Rebuild World
Record of Wortenia War*
Reincarnated as the Piggy Duke: This Time I'm Gonna Tell Her How I Feel!
The Saga of Lioncourt**
Seirei Gensouki: Spirit Chronicles
Seventh
The Skull Dragon's Precious Daughter**
Slayers
Sometimes Even Reality Is a Lie!*
Sorcerous Stabber Orphen*
Sweet Reincarnation**
The Tales of Marielle Clarac*
Tearmoon Empire*
To Another World... with Land Mines!
The Unwanted Undead Adventurer*
VTuber Legend: How I Went Viral after Forgetting to Turn Off My Stream
Welcome to Japan, Ms. Elf!*
When Supernatural Battles Became Commonplace
The Wind That Reaches the Ends the World**
The World's Least Interesting Master Swordsman
Yashiro-kun's Guide to Going Solo
Yuri Tama: From Third Wheel to Trifecta

...and more!
* Novel and Manga Editions
** Manga Only
Keep an eye out at j-novel.club for further new title announcements!